From the Library of

_____

GIVING BACK WITH PURPOSE

Fueling growth through community involvement

Giving Back With Purpose: Fueling Growth through Community Involvement
Copyright © 2013 by Main Street Books
All rights reserved.

Published by Main Street Books.
For more information contact mainstreetj11@gmail.com

ISBN# 978-0-9890173-1-2

Cover picture by Donny Granger of Creation Studios Gallery, as part of the Memphis Collection benefiting MPD Fallen Officer Memorial.

Printed in the United States of America

GIVING BACK WITH
PURPOSE

Fueling growth through community involvement

By **Jeremy Park** *Forword by* **Johnny Pitts**

As Governor, I have the privilege of seeing a lot of the great gatherings around the state of Tennessee. The Lipscomb Pitts Breakfast Club is a place where members of the community come together to hear examples of the many great things happening in Memphis. I appreciate the LPBC and the impact it makes on Memphis.

Tennessee Governor Bill Haslam

Lipscomb Pitts Breakfast Club is redefining the business consciousness of its city…it's an amazingly thin place where Business Intersects with Purpose to fuel community transformation. Seeing first-hand the collaboration between community and business leaders through hands-on SERVICE to inject HOPE into the lives of the most vulnerable of their city in the most truest form of humility, is truly a sight to behold…I'm convinced that the LPBC model for community transformation should be duplicated by other cities as a catalyst for putting a new face to what SERVANT LEADERSHIP should look like for a healthy city. This book is a must read for any business looking to transform its community through collaboration…

Manny Ohonme, Founder of Samaritans Feet

ACKNOWLEDGEMENTS

This book is a testament to teamwork and the countless people who have blessed me with their mentorship, friendship, and trust.

Although I am rarely too outward in my expression of faith, God is the anchor for me and my family. Each night we pray for strength, health, and guidance, so that we can do the things that need to be done on this earth to honor Him. I view our work with the Lipscomb Pitts Breakfast Club as a responsibility, so when we talk about helping others and making the Mid-South a place our kids are proud to call home, faith and family play an integral role, at least for me personally.

My wife, Meredith, and two sons, Cooper and Cayson, are my personal prides and source of support and encouragement. Honestly, the work I do would not be possible without the help of my wife, who is my best friend and rock. She graciously allows me the freedom to view what I do as a calling versus a job and forgives me for not being cognizant of the clock many days of the week. Yes, she has earned her angel wings! My parents, Julie and John, instilled the values of community service and are role models, like my brother, Jeff. My wife's side of the family is also engaged in the community, so I am happy to say that I am surrounded by compassionate and loving family that care deeply about others and our homeland. So, the first thank you goes to God and my family, who provide the foundation to make this work possible.

The next thank you goes to my co-workers at Lipscomb & Pitts Insurance, all of the amazing partners of the Lipscomb Pitts Breakfast Club, and the truly countless friends that we interact with across the Mid-South. This includes all of the nonprofit, business, government, and education leaders, who are all doing so much good. This book is a culmination and celebration of your engagement and efforts in the community, including that of your time, talents, treasure, and leadership that you so generously give back to help others. You are friends and mentors and together we are rolling up our sleeves to serve and give back. I love what we are doing and am proud of the impact we are having as a team!

Speaking of team, I want to thank Johnny Pitts, who believed in me from the start and gave me the chance to forge such a philanthropic path with our organization. It is an honor working for you, Johnny, Mat Lipscomb III, Lipscomb & Pitts Insurance, and the Lipscomb Pitts Breakfast Club. I appreciate your vision and trust, as we originally ventured out into things, like a weekly newspaper column, radio show, television show, screening at a film festival, and now a book. Allison Carson deserves much credit and thanks, as well, as she not only works tirelessly as my right hand to help organize all of our events and efforts, but also does things like build our LPBC website from scratch, so we can be more efficient. It always takes a village and we are blessed with an all-star team in Allison Carson, Nicole Blum, and Rehana Hanley, who make it look so easy! Thanks, team!

This book would also not be possible without James Overstreet, who originally presented the idea of writing the "Giving Back" column back in 2009. The column kicked off in 2010 and it was wonderful working with James and the Memphis Daily News team. In early 2013, we had a tremendous opportunity to move the column to The Commercial Appeal and have it published in their Sunday edition, as well as their free Thursday weeklies. Thank you to George Cogswell and Paul Jewell for sharing the vision and supporting both the Lipscomb Pitts Breakfast Club and the "Giving Back" column. It has been a pleasure working with you and your Commercial Appeal team. Many more great days are ahead as we continue to celebrate those individuals and organizations leading by example and foster and encourage more community engagement.

Just as important, I want to thank Jonathan Lindberg and his team at Main Street Books. Jonathan presented the idea of compiling these "Giving Back" columns into a book and his team worked hard to update statistics, gather quotes, and give this book a life of its own. Thank you for your vision, help, and guidance, as this book hopefully will inspire individuals to get more involved in their hometown.

I know I am forgetting so many friends, like Anthony Cava and Brian Leinbach, mentors, like my coaches and teachers, and individuals, like Merv Grifin, Dick Clark, and Cindy Clark, who have played an important role in my life and the work we are doing in the community. My life is a direct reflection of your sharing your time and wisdom. Just know I greatly appreciate everything you have done and continue to do for me and our community!

DEDICATION

This book is dedicated to God, my family, and those who have and continue to play an integral role in my life. It is dedicated first to my beautiful and brilliant wife, Meredith, who continues each day to hold my hand and serve as an inspiration and source of strength for me and our family. It is for our two boys, Cooper and Cayson, who make me proud to be a father and will one day carry the torch of leading our family and doing their part to make a difference in our great city and nation. Boys, Meredith and I love you more than anything!

This book is also dedicated to my parents, John and Julie, who are role models and have always supported me and my brother, instilling in us a responsibility to help others and give back. Similarly, it is for Meredith's parents, Kay and John Hussey, and her side of the family, who continue to lift us with love and support.

This book is dedicated my brother, Jeff, who proudly serves our country as an officer in the Marines. Although geography may separate us as you do your job, you are always in my heart and on my mind. Be safe and know we love you, your wife, Rachel, and son, Thomas (TW)! God bless you and all the other brave men and women who serve our country!

To the rest of my family, including Aunt Sandy, Aunt Nancy, Uncle Ned, and all of my cousins, nieces, and nephews, know that

GIVING BACK WITH PURPOSE

I love you and appreciate your love and support. To Aunt Diane, Uncle Tommy, and Uncle Roger, you were centers of our family and we miss you as you shine down from Heaven.

Lastly, this book is dedicated to anyone who is searching for their way to give back, make their mark, and transform this world for the betterment of all.

TABLE OF CONTENTS

FOREWORD

When I hear the term "Giving Back," I automatically assume that something was given in the first place, which requires giving back. In the case of so many stories in this book, the people and companies who are giving back are the recipients of the gift of extraordinary leadership, unique corporate culture, and loyal community support. As citizens in a thriving city, like Memphis, which is located in the growing south — a major region of the world's most enduring capitalistic country — we are also the recipients of great things, simply because of where we live.

Americans are better off than any other nationality in the world. That can be measured in several ways, but it is difficult to disagree with that general statement. One major reason that we are better off is because there is something in the DNA of Americans that gives us the desire to help those who are less fortunate, those who are down and out, and those who need help. This unique strain of American DNA helps create a feeling of community support to help those in need. In other words, one reason we are better off is because we can count on each other.

Think about it. We live in a country with a built-in, automatic relief system that does not have to be passed by Congress. It is fascinating....really. For example, whenever there is a natural disaster and families are in need, something interesting and unexpected happens. Americans rally to help and you could not stop them if you tried. The "giver" feels as good as the one who is receiving the gift of help and does not expect anything in return.

But "giving back" has transformed and evolved far beyond the natural disasters. It is no longer a reactive impulse, but rather a proactive plan to help. Just a decade or two ago, it was normal corporate behavior to give money to various causes, i.e. nonprofits, because it was the right thing to do. Now, we see companies not only writing the checks, but also interacting with nonprofits to guide them to success. This more hands-on approach is different.

It is not unusual to see the C-Suite personally plug into a nonprofit and then see their employee staff follow them. After all the checks have cleared, the people still remain actively engaged, which is where the real action begins and the results take form.

Today's Millennials are not only searching for a job, but also for meaning. They view their company as a means to get more engaged in their community. The interviewer becomes the interviewee as these young folks ask questions like, how does your company give back and what is your corporate protocol for employee involvement with nonprofits? The answers to these questions may very well be the deciding point between your talented new hire or the near miss.

Community involvement is not just the right thing to do, it is also the smart thing to do. Business owners want good, productive employees and having a mechanism in place for them to be involved in the community with their fellow workers creates a common cause beyond the scope of the paycheck. They can work together as a team to do something that, perhaps, they could not have done on their own.

Along the way, something happens. Friendships are created, not just with co-workers, but also with employees of other companies. Thus, a natural network is born which takes on a much deeper relationship than a one hour business lunch. This is where the American DNA thrives.

Memphis and our Lipscomb Pitts Breakfast Club are micro labs of this concept. We are, after all, one of the most giving cities in America. Giving back is a defining trait of our soul and culture, not just individually, but also corporately. This book exemplifies and summarizes many of these stories and opportunities and may just give you some ideas as to how you can make a difference in the lives of others. Wouldn't it be great to have that sort of legacy and be known for something like that?

Johnny Pitts
Lipscomb & Pitts Insurance
October, 2013

Chapter 1

A PRELUDE

Giving back and helping others has always been a big part of my life. Growing up, my family had an open door policy for those who might have been down on their luck, needed some advice or encouragement, or had a challenge that required additional resources. It was not out of the ordinary for my younger brother, Jeff, and I to be playing outside or around the house and, at any hour of the day, find ourselves playing with other kids, whose families were there visiting with our parents.

My father, John, and mother, Julie, are hardworking parents that want the best for their family, friends, and community. Like other parents, they put aside many of their own ambitions, in order to be there for me and my brother with unconditional love, supporting us on a number of crazy adventures along the way. They are role models in showing the power of servant leadership and how treating everyone with upmost respect and the best of intentions helps everyone succeed. My parents also instilled a mindset to focus on positive energy, to be a part of the solution by being an "upstander" versus a bystander, to work hard and never give up, dream big while having faith, and to understand our responsibility and the importance of service to God, our family, our environment and humankind.

When we showed interest in the Boy Scouts of America, they stepped up and poured their souls into not only building the character of their own two sons, but of hundreds of others, as well. Looking back, I have many fond memories of community service projects, summer camps, trips to Philmont Scout Ranch, and, of course, selling Trails End popcorn. Although I cannot remember all the knots, I can still recite the Scout Oath, Code, and Promise. More importantly, I am still applying many of the leadership lessons I originally learned as a Boy Scout. Although tennis ultimately took me in a different direction, I am proud to say that my brother, now a distinguished Marine serving our country, is an Eagle Scout and my parents, still both heavily involved in Scouting, have impacted the lives of thousands of men, at this point. And, yes, their home still maintains an open door policy.

The irony for me is that my father worked in the insurance industry, but I really never paid much attention to it. Like most kids, I was more concerned that he would play with me, watch me practice, or root me on as I competed in all of the tennis tournaments. Even in college, as a Marketing Major, I was more focused on being creative and learning how to position and leverage available resources for the greatest impact, versus showing interest in an industry my father felt I might appreciate. Today, it brings us both a smile to know that my work in community engagement and corporate philanthropy is fueled through an insurance agency, Lipscomb & Pitts Insurance, LLC. Lipscomb & Pitts is the Mid-South's largest independent insurance agency and one of the largest in the nation. I am proud to be a Vice President and Member of the LLC with the agency, just as much as I am to serve as the President of the Lipscomb Pitts Breakfast Club.

The story of the Lipscomb Pitts Breakfast Club (LPBC) and the experiences and lessons that have shaped and led us to where we are today is a fun conversation, but not the subject of this book. What you do need to know, though, is that our organization is a privately-funded catalyst for the Mid-South. A team of team of partner businesses, comprised of some of the largest and most influential employers in the world to mid-size and smaller local firms, have come together to align resources for philanthropic efforts and to underwrite the cost of around 150 events each year to enrich leaders and impact our community.

Strategically, we are focused on five key areas: 1) Bringing corporations together to focus on collective impact in the community; 2) Bringing all four quadrants of our city — business, nonprofit, education, and government — together to foster collaboration; 3) Making it easy for all citizens to become more engaged by offering FREE public events that offer enrichment and give back; 4) Providing a pipeline for positive stories to be shared and media outlets to spread good news and energy; and 5) Providing turnkey, easy opportunities for companies and their employees to become more engaged in the community.

So, we host tons of seminars and workshops, coordinate weekly executive lunches, bring in national guest speakers with our Signature Breakfast Series, and put together a variety of other events to provide valuable content and foster teamwork and collaboration among business and city leaders. We then provide turnkey opportunities for companies and individuals to become more engaged in the community and leverage collective resources to make an impact through volunteer days, action projects, nonprofit tours, fundraising, and more. Recent examples include tutoring after school, mentoring, scrubbing graffiti off buildings and bridges, washing the feet of over 2,000 kids and providing them with new socks and shoes, helping to pick up 34,000 pounds of trash from McKellar Lake and the Mississippi River, spearheading the Memphis Police Department Fallen Officer Memorial, creating and promoting the Power of the Dollar Campaign ("buy local"), launching a civic pride effort called "Memphis Rocks," and hosting a telethon.

We author a free weekly email newsletter for the community that is filled with positive news and lists all of our upcoming LPBC events open to the public, job postings, nonprofit events, and much more. Taking our focus on sharing positive stories and promoting engagement opportunities within the community to an even broader audience, we have a weekly newspaper column, a weekly radio show, and a monthly television series. Our LPBC Radio Show airs each Saturday from 1:00p to 2:00p on News Radio 600 WREC. Our television show, The SPARK, airs the third Thursday of each month at 9:00p on WKNO-TV. Then, each Sunday our "Giving Back" column is published in The Commercial Appeal. The column spotlights the efforts of local nonprofits and offers creative ways to weave giving back into your normal life and business routine. The column is also featured each Thursday in their Weeklies, which are freely distributed to households across the Mid-South.

I started writing the "Giving Back" column in 2010 and, to date, have had the pleasure of spotlighting well over a hundred nonprofits, corporations, and individuals leading by example. Likewise, we have covered some amazing efforts and initiatives, along with philanthropic trends and helpful tips to make giving back easy. I want to thank James Overstreet with the Memphis Daily News, who originally approached me with the idea of writing the column and gave me the opportunity and freedom to take it in different directions, all with a positive theme focused on increasing community engagement. The "Giving Back" column was published weekly in both the Memphis Daily News and Memphis News from 2010 to early 2013, when we had the opportunity to take it in a new direction with The Commercial Appeal. I want to personally thank George Cogswell, Publisher, and Paul Jewell, Marketing Director, of The Commercial Appeal for believing in and supporting the LPBC and the "Giving Back" column. They have provided a tremendous platform by publishing the column in their Sunday papers and then again in their free Weeklies. It is truly an amazing opportunity and I am extremely grateful.

Finally, that brings us to this book. After three years of weekly columns, we have covered quite a range with the "Giving Back" column. Thanks to Jonathan Lindberg and his team at Main Street Books, we thought it would be fun, but also helpful to pull together some of our favorites and compile them in a book. These columns cover corporations leading by example, nonprofits doing amazing work and easy ways to help their efforts, reader responses and a whole chapter on why Memphis Rocks, and some of my personal perspectives. We have gone back and updated all of the statistics, collected quotes from many different local leaders, and added some new material to give this book a life of its own. The best part, though, is keeping true to everything we do with the LPBC — where we weave giving back into every event and effort — this book, itself, is 100 percent a give back. All proceeds from the book will be used to purchase books for local schools in need. So, it is a book about giving back that gives back by buying books for students to learn!

To me, this book and what it stands for perfectly sums up my philosophy that we can make giving back easy and weave it into our normal routine. The key is to be intentional by adding an extra layer to the things you are already doing, so there is "Purpose." When you look at the traditional marketing mix model, it always includes the four P's of Product, Price, Place, Promotion, and then sometimes also includes People, Process, and Position. The next evolution will include "Purpose." It has made national headlines, but consumers are now looking at corporate America to be a part of the solution, which means they are more strongly considering a company's community efforts and impact when making their purchasing decisions. Stated differently and borrowing a quote by Brent Bushnell in a recent Forbes column by Evan Kirkpatrick, Brent states "Companies without social impact culture will soon be obsolete."

We will cover it in later chapters, but the trend in corporate philanthropy centers around engagement and getting employees more involved by lending their time, talents, expertise, and resources to give back. We have also seen the rise of philanthropic capitalism with the popularity of one-for-one companies, like Toms shoes or Warby Parker that donate a pair of shoes or pair of eye glasses respectively for each purchase made by a consumer. While the one-for-one model is definitely a game changer for social impact, I realize that it is not realistic for all companies. What is realistic, though, is finding and adding a higher purpose and realizing that together we really can create change to strengthen and benefit our community.

My hope is that you enjoy reading this book and learn more about the heartfelt efforts taking place each day here in the Mid-South. There are countless people who are leading by example and we applaud and appreciate their efforts! I also hope that you are inspired by what you read and will take a next step of getting more engaged, perhaps with one of the nonprofits highlighted, or starting your own effort. As an aside, you will find that giving back can be a very powerful growth strategy for yourself, your family, and your business. Movements start with small actions and you will be surprised at what you can accomplish by just doing three things each day that either helps someone or helps our community. Indeed, there is no better time than now to start fueling growth — your personal development, professional momentum, and community success — by focusing on engagement and purpose. So, enjoy the book, stay in touch with your stories and successes, and let us work together to make our city, region, and nation even greater tomorrow than it is today!

CORPORATE THEMED

Chapter 2

PARTNERSHIPS KEY IN BAPTIST OPERATION OUTREACH

Regarded as one of the most premier health care systems in the nation, Baptist Memorial Health Care is an award-winning network dedicated to providing compassionate, high-quality care for patients. Since their modest beginning in 1912 with a 150-bed hospital, Baptist has grown to 14 affiliate hospitals throughout the Mid-South in order to meet the expanding needs of our community. The same caring atmosphere and mission that inspired the founders continues today to lead every aspect of operation at Baptist.

One of my favorite sides to Baptist is their community efforts and collaborative nature to giving back. Through Baptist Operation Outreach, for example, they are teaming with Christ Community Health Services to reach beyond the walls of their hospitals and provide free health care to more than 3,000 homeless patients a year. Free primary medical, dental, and vision care is provided five days a week. Their clinic is located in Midtown at Jefferson and Cleveland and on Mondays you can find them at Memphis Union Mission. They have expanded service with an additional site at Salvation Army. Recently, they unveiled their new mobile unit, which will help increase capacity even further.

At Baptist Memorial Health Care, we believe in the three-fold ministry of Christ: healing, preaching and teaching. With that as our mission, our outreach extends beyond the walls of our 14 hospitals. Our work serving the homeless through our mobile clinic, women by offering mobile mammography, special-needs children through building classrooms, our community by giving free heart-risk assessments and continual outreach to our patient population shows just a few of the ways we are committed to the future of health care for our region.

Scott Fountain, Baptist Memorial Health Care

Baptist partnered to create the Bellevue Baptist Christian Mobile Dental Clinic, which goes to churches throughout the community in underserved areas. Dentists volunteer to help provide free dental care to families and individuals who have little or no access to dental care. Since its inception in 2008, the dental van has served over 7,500 individuals. Recognizing the need to provide vision care and eyeglasses, so children and adults can see clearly at school and apply for jobs, Baptist partnered yet again. Southern College of Optometry verifies initial screenings conducted in the clinic and writes prescriptions, which are then filled by Davis Vision to provide free eyeglasses.

Teamed with the health care, Baptist has a partnership with the Community Alliance for the Homeless, which helps families and individuals find permanent housing. This holistic and collaborative approach is a perfect example of the power of partnerships. With more families and children now living on the streets, the face of homelessness has changed. It is critical for us, as a community, to support and foster even more of this teamwork in order to transform our city.

Chapter 3

DATA FACTS LEADING BY EXAMPLE

Typically, when "corporate philanthropy" was mentioned in the past, the term was tied to financial contributions aimed at helping nonprofits and improving the community. Now, however, that term has taken on a much larger meaning by focusing on engagement. The trend has made front page headlines recently with consumers noting that a company's engagement and goodwill is quickly becoming a more prominent part of their purchasing decision. Employees, especially Millenials, likewise, are now selecting employers based on engagement offerings.

Ken Gladdish, President and CEO of the Seton Foundations, recently talked in Memphis about these trends and the Social Framework of Generosity. Part of his presentation focused on the breakdown in teaching and exemplifying philanthropy. Based on a number of different factors, philanthropy is not being taught as much at the kitchen table, on the playing field, or in the sanctuary, classroom, clubhouse, or town hall. So, companies must start filling that gap from an engagement, training and education, and leadership role.

The exciting news is that each day, more citizens and corporations around the Mid-South are raising their hands to be a part of the solution. One such company is Data Facts, a 24 year old, local company that provides background screening and lending solution needs to businesses around the nation. Their President and CEO, Daphne

Large, is heavily involved in our community and is an example of the power in modeling the way and inspiring a shared vision.

> *We believe that to whom much has been given, much is expected. This notion has been a guiding principle at Data Facts from our Management team and throughout all of our associates. By donating our time, treasures and talents to several worthwhile and extraordinary non-profits, we know that we have helped make a difference in the communities we serve.*
>
> Daphne Large, Data Facts

Data Facts financially supports many organizations and raises the bar on personal engagement. Their team recently put together and hosted a 600 egg Easter Egg Hunt for children at Youth Villages. For Valentine's Day, they deliver cupcakes to children and for Christmas, their employees contribute money, shop for gifts, wrap them, and throw parties to deliver the presents to kids across the Mid-South. Their team organized a six month food drive for the Mid-South Food Bank and worked hard physically stocking the shelves. They help build Habitat for Humanity homes, send employees to elementary schools to provide books and read to students, and purchase and install air conditioners for elderly families in need over the summer.

This is just a small sample that exemplifies how Data Facts is making it easy and fun for their team to make a difference. Many then serve on boards and are further individually engaged in the community. The key is realizing that while money is a great resource, people are the real problem solvers and drivers of success for a city. Thus, it is critical for each of us to play our part!

Chapter 4

POWER OF A MEMPHIS DOLLAR

Each year, Lipscomb & Pitts asks different leaders in Memphis where they see opportunities to to strengthen our city. Back in 2010, the prominent theme was dollars flowing out of Memphis. Story after story focused on local companies, large and small, not being given a chance to bid or work on local projects. From a city-wide perspective, we felt a strong need to raise the awareness on the caliber of companies we enjoy in the Mid-South, as well as the economic impact created when we spend our dollars locally.

From a business lens, we have global leaders, innovators, and famous entrepreneurs that are proud to call Memphis home. We have jewels — large, mid-size, and small — that are every bit as talented and creative as what you would find in cities like Los Angeles, Dallas, Chicago, or New York. Personally, I can attest since I have lived and worked in quite a few of these cities.

> *"Community service has been a long standing part of our culture at Yuletide. We make it a goal to give at least 9% of our net profits back to the numerous organizations that work so hard to improve the lives of so many in our community. Whether through monetary gifts, volunteering for events, or donation of goods and services, Yuletide is a company that is committed to giving back."*
>
> Chris Miller, Yuletide Office Solutions

Being local, our companies are able to provide face-to-face customer service with the ability to take responsibility and action at odd hours of the day or night, if needed. It gives me comfort to know that if an issue arises, it can be addressed quickly without much effort on my end. So, one of our key duties is to raise awareness for our city's talented companies and creating referral networks, so that whatever product or service you need, we can direct you to the best fit.

Economically, we found that every dollar spent locally creates $1.70 in economic impact for Memphis. We also found that every $1 million helps create 11 new jobs. We used these as the foundation for a PSA-type approach to raising awareness, dubbed the Power of the Dollar campaign.

The goal is to plant the seed that there are valid business and economic reasons to first look locally with needed products and services. It is proven that cities with a "Buy Local First" campaign enjoy higher growth rates, productivity and pride.

The next step is to do an internal audit and see what percentage, outside of payroll, your company spends locally. At Lipscomb & Pitts Insurance, we found that 78% of our dollars were spent locally and have pledged each year to seek to raise that percentage. By focusing on raising that percentage, we are now placing a higher priority on the value of being local. I encourage you to conduct your own internal audit and join the pledge to increase your percentage of local purchases.

Chapter 5

LATE BLOOMERS

Giving back is not just something nonprofits, churches and philanthropists are doing. Hundreds of businesses are giving back every day across Memphis. It is wonderful to watch when a business develops a heart for investing in the community. It is a commitment not just to selling or manufacturing — it is all about using the power of business to reinvest in the city where we live. The impact is immeasurable!

One such story popped up on my computer screen from LPBC partner Mike Bowen, CEO and President of Champion Awards & Apparel. The story is about "late bloomers" and is a testament for how businesses can play an active role in the community and how someone's past does not have to predict his or her future.

Mike Bowen: 'Not long ago, a customer (let's call him John) asked me to interview a man who we will call 'Sam". John allows Sam to live in one of his rental houses, rent-free. John pays Sam's utilities because he has no job or means to obtain one. You see, Sam is a felon. Champion hired Sam because we believe felons are people too. Sam has successfully completed a month of learning how to print T-shirts. He gets up every morning at 4:00am and rides the bus to our factory.

John asked me "Why do you think we help people who sometimes can't help themselves?" I thought about it before responding, "We help because it makes us feel good to do what our parents or grandparents did. They gave us a chance to fail and still loved us. Most of these folks didn't have that."

Champion Awards and Apparel aims to improve the quality of life in our community — to help the folks that help others. Since 2007 , we have trained over 100 Late Bloomers on a part time basis and presently have 9 full time Late Bloomers on staff. They are some of our best team members.

Mike Bowen, Champion Awards and Apparel

When my mom called four years ago and asked me to consider hiring felons right out of prison, I thought she was crazy. She had begun teaching business skills to prisoners. Yes, at almost seventy-two years young, each month, she drives to a high security prison in Whiteville, TN, Forrest City, Arkansas, or Tiptonville, TN at 6:00am…She is escorted through a maze of security checkpoints to a room of up to eighty felons, all trying to get parole. She teaches each class for at least four hours. She began this program through her association with SCORE and is changing lives.

Through her teachings, Mom met Patrick and asked me to hire him. I was extremely skeptical, but she explained the Transitions Ministries program. Men with certain felonies must qualify for parole by living in a halfway program for a minimum amount of time….This program transports late bloomers to and from work. If a particular late bloomer doesn't bloom, they are not asked back… Champion now has six successful, fulltime late bloomers.

Oh, and for Patrick, he's my hero! He has been with us for over three years. He is our Warehouse Manager and a real leader. He has a beautiful daughter, girlfriend, home, and car and is a proud late bloomer."

How you can give back: There are thousands of late bloomers in this community just looking for chance. Consider giving Transition Ministries a call at 901-414-9267 or visiting their website, www.forgivenesshouse.org.

Chapter 6

SERVICEMASTER MAKES MEMPHIS ROCK

All around Memphis, individuals and businesses are giving back, each in their own way. Their stories are our stories. Businesses of all sizes, large and small, are spearheading hands-on campaigns to make a difference. We see Memphians taking pride in their city, showing how Memphis rocks! We see nonprofits working behind the scenes to impact our city in a positive way.

I would like to share with you a small story of how people in Memphis are giving back in a big way. One day, we received a call from Buddy Chapman with CrimeStoppers, who had received a SeniorBsafe tip regarding an elderly couple whose house was badly infested with cockroaches. The situation was direr because the husband suffers from dementia and is not able to clearly communicate while the wife is bedridden and unable to move due to a recent stroke. Buddy had inspected the home and was shocked to find the infestation was so severe that cockroaches were crawling all over the woman, who was not able to react. Buddy realized the couple needed immediate help and, unfortunately, faced financial challenges.

Thanks to Beth Flanagan with Memphis Medical Center and Jeff Fedorchak at ServiceMaster, we were able to quickly send the couple's situation to Terminix, which is a ServiceMaster company. Terminix instantly sent out a crew to assess the situation and start treatment on the home. Their team even helped the elderly couple temporarily relocate to their son's house, so Terminix could do a thorough job.

> *"At ServiceMaster, giving back is a not just a commitment, it's a privilege. ServiceMaster has a long tradition of service in the community. We're proud to be a community partner and truly believe that our service can make a real difference in the lives of others."*
>
> Peter Tosches, ServiceMaster

While treating the house, Terminix branch manager Kenny Diotte and his team uncovered significant plumbing problems and contacted one of their long-time contractors, Crosswind Construction, to do the repair work for free. Merry Maids, another ServiceMaster brand, heard about the couple's situation and volunteered to thoroughly clean their home. Terminix has continued to service the home and will do so, until the problem is completely eradicated. All of this was done at no cost to the family, as a way of helping a family in need.

The act of kindness brought tears of appreciation to the elderly couple's eyes, but it also brought tears of joy to those that helped. Christina Bowman, Merry Maids branch manager said, "When I shared this couple's story with my team, I had 10 associates volunteer to help out. They related the situation to if it was their parents or grandparents in this unfortunate situation and how they would want someone to help their families. It was emotional for my team and me to be at the home and know the homeowner's situation. It meant a lot to us to help Memphis neighbors in such need."

This is a perfect example of the heartwarming moments and community collaborations where people are helping people each day in our community. We applaud these everyday heroes, like those at ServiceMaster and SeniorBsafe, who make Memphis rock!

Chapter 7

HOLIDAY SAFETY TIPS

Memphis comes alive during the holiday season. Theatre Memphis provides holiday cheer with its telling of A Christmas Carol. The Brooks Museum lets you find your inner child as you build a gingerbread house. Afterward, you can step outside and take a carriage ride through Overton Park. Or if you want to see 'Memphis snow', head over to the Botanic Gardens and wander through the festive My Big Backyard.

The city comes alive during the holiday season. Christmastime also kicks the holiday shopping season into high-gear, which can bring its own risks and its own rewards. Staying safe during the holiday bustle takes just a little extra awareness. There is always a traditional spike in crime, but petty crime does not have to affect you.

Thanks to the Phelps family, who own Phelps Security and organize a community action group known as B.I.G. for Memphis (Business Interest Group), we are armed with resources. The group hosts monthly meetings that bring business leaders together with Colonels from the Memphis Police Department for abbreviated Blue CRUSH presentations and to share information and helpful crime prevention tips. Below are some tips from the MPD Colonels that will help us to be safer this holiday season.

"Phelps Security gives back every day. We work to bring community business leaders together to learn about the positive things being done in our community to fight crime."

Patti Phelps, Phelps Security

Lock your car doors and keep your windows rolled up while pumping gas. Ladies, instead of leaving your purse in the passenger seat, hide it or place it under your seat. Thieves are opening car doors and stealing purses while women are pumping gas. They are also working in pairs, so as one distracts you, the other reaches into your car.

Hide all belongings BEFORE you get to the store or destination. Thieves are watching as you arrive, so if you try to hide your personal artifacts then, it may be too late. Avoid dropping off shopping bags and re-entering stores for the same reason. Make sure to park in a well-lit area, near people, and remember to stash things like cords and mounts with your iPods and GPS systems.

When exercising at a gym, carry your keys with you versus leaving them in a locker. Criminals are getting into the lockers, grabbing your keys, clicking the alarm to find your car, then stealing it.

Keep your home well lit and bushes trimmed near doors and in front of windows. Avoid placing your Christmas tree in front of a window, which showcases presents. If traveling, have neighbors pick up your mail and paper. Report any suspicious vehicles to your precinct.

Keeping your business tidy and clean deters crime. Two employees should open and close your store. Test your alarm and surveillance cameras to make sure they work. Lastly, ladies, if someone does try to grab your purse, throw your purse the opposite direction and run away. Almost always, the thief will go toward the purse, giving you time to flee. Just make sure you have copies of your credit cards at home.

These tips apply to everyone, everywhere and not just in Memphis. I encourage you to help spread the word and let us work together to keep our community safe during the holiday season.

Chapter 8

SUPPORT THE MPD FALLEN OFFICER MEMORIAL

In Memphis, we are always learning about heroes. We see them in our schools, giving back their time and energy to invest in our future. We watch them in our hospitals and clinics, developing new ways to save and extend our quality of life. And, of course, heroes are on our streets every day, our firefighters and police officers, putting their lives on the line in order to protect ours.

While many large metropolitans have monuments for their Fallen and we have the Fire Museum of Memphis for our local Firefighter heroes, up until now, Memphis has never had a monument to honor its Memphis Police Department Fallen Officers and the families and friends they leave behind. There are currently 2,400 officers and civilians working with the MPD, which has a rich legacy dating back to 1827. The number of officers, who have lost their lives in the line of duty, over the last 186 years, currently totals 62.

"The memorial honors officers killed in the line of duty and gives their families a place to remember and reflect on their sacrifice. Citizens are given a chance to make the memorial possible and feel a connection to the officers who gave their all for our community"

Jim Tusant, Memphis/Shelby County
Law Enforcement Foundation

Each of us on the committee feels honored and humbled to even have an opportunity to play a part in this effort. I have many friends who serve our community every day, as a part of the MPD "Blue." I have family, including a younger brother, in the military, who risk their lives to protect the freedoms of our great nation. I know all too well the feeling of worry and helplessness that engulfs your life while a loved one is placed in harm's way. While my brother was over in Afghanistan, our family prayed all day, every day, and counted down the minutes until his return. So, my heart goes out to all of the men and women who sacrifice their lives for our cities and nation. As a father, my heart also goes out to their children.

A retired MPD Colonel provided the original vision of this monument, from the centerpiece to the prominent and family-friendly location at the Oak Court Mall. The statue depicts a male and female officer presenting the flag of a Fallen to a child. It is heartwarming reminder of the price that is paid each day in Memphis for our safety and protection.

How you can give back: The Memphis Police Department Fallen Officer Memorial is 100 percent privately funded. It is one way to honor those Officers who have given their lives to protect our city and recognize the daily efforts of our Memphis Police Department.

Learn more about the project and consider contributing to the effort through the Memphis/Shelby County Law Enforcement Foundation at www.MSCLEfoundation.org.

MEMPHIS THEMED

Chapter 9

WHAT MEMPHIS MEANS TO YOU

Memphis pride is GROWING! Memphis means so many things to so many different people — the city shines in a unique way. If I were to ask you the question, "What does Memphis mean to you?" how you would respond?

This question has taken on a new meaning for me over the last few years. It has been amazing to witness the reaction of guest speakers that we bring in for LPBC events. They are so moved by our warm hospitality, genuine nature, sense of values, and dedication to community, that they have become our friends and champions for Memphis, in the process.

Manny Ohonme, founder of Samaritan's Feet, travels the world and sets Memphis as the example of how leaders can come together, humble themselves, and wash the feet of impoverished children, providing them with new shoes and renewed hope. Richard Sheirer, who was in charge of the 9-11-01 cleanup in New York City, was so moved by Memphis that he sent us the flag that flew over New York, commemorating the 10th Anniversary of the three attacks on our country. Digger Phelps spent 45 minutes talking on national television about his trip to Memphis and the Stax Music Academy.

In so many ways, Memphis is a rich city. We are rich in compassion. We are rich in charitable contributions, and we are rich in volunteerism. The Lipscomb Pitts Break-

fast Club develops those assets. They are a vital resource, which brings the community together. I'm excited that they have chosen to share their efforts and successes in this new book, Giving Back.

Mayor Mark Luttrell, Shelby County Mayor

These speakers, who travel all over the world, are spreading "Memphis Love." Recently, we started capturing these testimonials to create an archive for everyone to see and share. We realized, in the process, that we need to do a better job of asking ourselves why we love our city and then sharing those moments, as well.

So, we have started recording interviews with various leaders, focused on the subject of Memphis. Our goal is to put together a narrative that will spotlight what makes our city so unique and special and to capture that spirit from Memphians themselves. So far, we have been blown away with heartfelt responses. There are many common themes, like home and family, big-city opportunities with small town values, world-class cultural arts, sports, the nation's largest urban park, top ranked zoo, short commute, fine dining, barbeque, music, and being one of the nation's most giving cities.

Having lived and worked in many large cities, I love and appreciate the Memphis charm, set of values, and support system that you do not find elsewhere. Every city has issues, but the difference lies in how the citizens come together to solve them. I am proud to say that Memphians are rolling up their sleeves and starting a movement. We are standing at the edge of a renaissance, as we align resources and set out to unleash our global power.

Chapter 10

MEMPHIANS DEFINING MEMPHIS

W hat does Memphis mean to you? All year, I have been asking that question and I have received an interesting and diverse group of answers. Each answer highlights the greatness of Memphis. Here a few below:

Paul Morris: "Memphis is the underdog that when you least expect it wins your heart. We come from behind and invent a new way of doing something, like Rock 'n' Roll or the self-serve grocery store or curing cancer in children. We don't brag or even think that much of ourselves. We're humble and we're real. We have an old soul that has been through much misery and is able to persist through much more. We are the Blues, enjoying our depths and keeping the beat going for a brighter future."

Ken Steorts: "Memphis means community. A city big enough to offer everything one desires and small enough to do it with a personal touch. Like we sit on the river with a front porch to gather. Memphis is at its best when we work cooperatively. Collaboration and giving is a hallmark of this great place. Other cities might be the formal dining room of music, but Memphis is the kitchen. And everyone wants to be in the kitchen."

Mary Nicole Blum: "To me, Memphis means opportunity. As a young adult, once set on moving out of Memphis in order to land a "decent" job out of college, I now see the opportunities here-for the "young and naive"—to pave the way for other young professionals who feel the same. There are opportunities for young adults to find jobs they love in Memphis and if we don't stay and use our crafts to mold this city, it will never reach its potential."

Shelley Baur: "Though not born here, Memphis means home, and I love living here. I love Memphis, with all of its faces of authenticity, soulfulness, great art forms in all shapes, colors, sizes (especially, the music!!)…. I love celebrating Memphis with friends near and far when pockets of excellence are highlighted in national media — like Booker T. Washington High School's recognition by President Barack Obama… I love [when our grandchildren] fall in love with the new playground at Shelby Farms…"

Chapter 11

CONTINUING TO DEFINE MEMPHIS

Let us remain focused on the question, "What does Memphis mean to you?" Readers of the "Giving Back" column shared their personal thoughts as we work to create a community narrative that will help us align efforts and market our city. Here is another batch of answers from Memphians working to make Memphis great.

Bruce Meisterman: "Memphis, more than any other place I've lived, is the most responsive to new ideas. Obviously some will be good or even great, other perhaps not as much. But, and this is the main thing here, you can get your ideas acted on and realized. In a very good sense, Memphis was Silicon Valley before Silicon Valley: ideas abounding...but with a greater variety of successes."

Hud Andrews: "I have lived in Memphis all but one of my 63 years. Memphis, to me, is the spirit and heart of her people. We are the city which survived the death of Dr. King to become far stronger and closer-knit than we were the day he died. I like to say that everyone in Memphis is just one degree of separation from everyone else. Memphis is Rhodes College and the U of M. It is Le Moyne-Owen struggling to survive in a very difficult economy. It is Tiger basketball and the resurgent Grizzlies. One day I hope it will be the home of a very good Tiger football program and a winning program at Rhodes. It is Beale Street, B. B. King, and Elvis."

Charli Sanders: "For a small-towner like me, Memphis is place for me to find the opportunity to grow. Nowhere else in the world can a person find the headquarters of numerous international businesses mixed with a southern accent. I love it! The best part is that community and business leaders want graduating college students to stay right here and make a life for themselves. Memphis writes its own rules when it comes to... everything! It is truly unique."

Eric Brey: "Opportunity. There is something about this city; not something you can easily identify but a feeling to the city that has been growing over the past few years. Call it culture, a vibe, a change in perspective that seems to be happening throughout the city. It's a felling that there is an opportunity for something great, if you (or we, as a city) reach out and grab it. It's almost impossible to put it into words but there is something about this city, an opportunity for those who want to pursue it."

Chapter 12

DEFINING MEMPHIS

As we wrap up this section and reader-response series, I have to admit that I was amazed at the answers I received from the question, "What does Memphis mean to you?" Memphians shared their personal thoughts on how they define our great city and truly did a tremendous job capturing the heart and soul of our community. Here are a few more colorful responses:

Michael Drake: "Memphis means entrepreneurial spirit to me. From our heritage of visionaries like Clarence Saunders, Kemmons Wilson and Fred Smith to current entrepreneurs in industries like healthcare and technology, Memphis pioneers have not only changed the world, but they have changed our community by their personal involvement. I think our people are different — engaged, hospitable and caring. We hear it from visitors all the time. Must be the vibe we have with the water, food, music and fun."

Kenneth Whalum, Jr: "I love living and working in Memphis because of our rich heritage of music and ministry. The same atmosphere that birthed Aretha Franklin, Booker T & The MG's, and Maurice White of Earth, Wind & Fire is still producing world-changers today. That's why I introduced the idea of creating the Memphis Academy of Musical Arts & Sciences to teach young people the business side of music as well as enhance their natural talents. Because of music, Memphis is on the come up!"

Abby Elzemeyer: "I love being able to call myself a Memphian and an artist. The arts in Memphis never cease to amaze me. With the growth of the Hatiloo Theater in the Theater District, Artspace meeting and designing space for artist, and organizations like ArtsMemphis tying them all together Memphis can only continue to make an impact in the arts world. It's a wonderful time to be involved and supporting the Arts in Memphis."

Kathryn Dewey: "As an Army wife and transplant to Memphis, I view Memphis as a city of service. People are always ready to help their neighbor."

Mike Bowen: "... Memphis means freedom. I was free to swim and fish the Nonconnah Creek in the 60's. In the 70's, I was free to attend Wooddale H.S. We ushered in bussing with little problems... and then on to Memphis State. In the 80's, I was free with my parents and brother to start several small companies and merge them into the family business. In the 90's, I was free to raise a family in the county.... In the 2000's, we were free to purchase a condo in downtown Memphis to enjoy the revival of South Main Art district, Beale Street, two great basketball teams and a baseball team.... In Memphis you have the freedom to grow, learn, work, play, and enjoy one of the greatest cities and all its surrounding counties in the world!..."

So, now it's your turn, what does Memphis mean to you?

Chapter 13

WHY MEMPHIS ROCKS

I love asking the question, Why do *you* think Memphis rocks? There is such diversity in the answer. Memphis is vibrant and exciting, it is rockin' and alive. Music, theatre, shopping, entertainment, recreation and the arts — there is something here for everyone.

It was exactly this kind of civic pride that served as the foundation for the "Memphis Rocks" campaign, an effort that strives to give back, supporting the Memphis Police Department (MPD) Fallen Officer Memorial. We teamed with Champion Awards and Apparel to design a "Memphis Rocks" T-shirt that is sure to spark conversation by listing some of the many things that make our city great. The campaign is a fun way for our city to come together, wear our Memphis pride, and say thanks to those who protect our freedoms. Shirts are available at www.MemphisRocksMerch.com.

Memphis is the cradle of all things sacred — from legendary streets and studios, to the tastes tying the Delta to global influences to stories rolling on the Mississippi River.
Kevin Kane, Memphis Convention & Visitors Bureau

All proceeds benefit the MPD Fallen Officer Memorial, which is a million dollar, privately funded project to honor the 62 Officers who lost their lives in the line of duty and the family and friends they leave behind. Since we currently do not have anything to honor their sacrifices, we feel this is a much needed project for our community. Also, since we want to show broad community support and appreciation, a "Memphis Rocks" shirt is the perfect way for everyone to get involved and be a part of bringing the memorial to fruition.

So, after defining what the shirt stands for, let us now discuss why "Memphis Rocks" and why this slogan is so appropriate for our city. Yes, it is true that other cities have claimed they "rock" and another city might be home to the Rock n' Roll Hall of Fame, but our city is famously known as the Home of the Blues and the BIRTHPLACE of Rock n' Roll! We are also world renowned for our Soul, including the Stax Museum of American Soul Music! So, there is definitely more than one way to Rock! Last we checked, Memphis is mentioned in more songs than any other city in the world and we have a long legacy of music icons with Memphis roots, like Elvis, Aretha Franklin, Al Green, Kirk Whalum, Jerry Lee Lewis, Isaac Hayes, and Justin Timberlake.

You might say "it is in our drinking water" (famous for its quality), but we are globally recognized for our entrepreneurialism, warm hospitality, food (of course, including BBQ), our culture and arts, and our values and spirit. We rock at business and logistics and we rock on the basketball court…. you get the idea.

How about you, why do you think Memphis Rocks?

Chapter 14

WHY MEMPHIS ROCKS, ACCORDING TO MEMPHIANS:
PART I

So, we just explained the backstory for the "Memphis Rocks" campaign and asked you, the reader, "Why do you think Memphis Rocks?" Over the years, we have been engaging readers in some reader-response columns asking them this same question. The responses we received were heartwarming stories, catchy slogans and fascinating perspectives that capture the essence of what makes Memphis so great.

Here are a few I would like to share:

Pam Weakley: "It's all about the B's — BBQ, Beale, Blues, Bridge, and Basketball!"

Jerome Robinson: "Memphis Rocks because on any given day the great people of Memphis are hard at work doing and giving for others! This really is an amazing town."

Jason Brooks: "I love the festivals, like Memphis in May, the RiverArts Fest, Greek Fest, Italian Fest, Africa in April, Crawfish Fest and the Indie Memphis Film Festival. Really cool with the diversity, music, food and thousands of people coming out to enjoy. Oh, I can't forget things like South Main Trolley Tour and the Peabody Rooftop Parties… so much fun to be had in this city!"

Joe Fracchia: "My top 5 reasons Memphis Rocks — 1) entrepreneurial spirit, 2) friendly, welcoming people, 3) our sports and music heritage, 4) The Memphis Zoo, 5) all our locally owned restaurants."

Allison Carson: "I think Memphis Rocks because of the green grass, blue skies, and the soul in the air. More importantly, I love the way the community rallies around a cause when there is a need. The spirit of giving in Memphis is unmatched and the social responsibility is changing the landscape of what will be our great history. There is a buzz in the air that is building up to a big boom and it's an exciting time to be here!"

Steven Ardel: "Here are five reasons why Memphis Rocks and stats to back it up — 1) Memphis has one of the quickest commutes to work in the nation, 2) Memphis was named one of the most fun cities in the nation by Portfolio.com, 3) CNBC.com ranked Memphis #2 in the nation this year for being a least-expensive city to live in, 4) we have world recognized arts, culture, and heritage, like the Brooks Museum of Art, Dixon Gallery and Gardens, Elvis Presley's Graceland, Ballet Memphis, National Civil Rights Museum, Rock 'n' Soul Museum, and Orpheum Theatre, and 5) we enjoy world-class sports in accessible environments, like with our Tennis Championships each February, the FedEx St. Jude Classic at TPC Southwind in June, the AutoZone Liberty Bowl, Memphis Redbirds, Tiger Basketball, and Memphis Grizzlies, which were just named Sport Team of the Year for the Beyond Sport Awards 2012. It's a proven fact that Memphis Rocks!"

Dan Marks: "The greenline/Shelby Park. It truly is phenomenal how much this city invests in public green spaces."

Chapter 15

WHY MEMPHIS ROCKS, ACCORDING TO MEMPHIANS:
PART II

I mentioned before that we had TONS of responses, to the question "Why do you think Memphis Rocks?" Let us continue with more artful narratives and feedback.

Stacy McCall: "Not only is Memphis a great place to stay, to play and to live, it's also a great place to grow a business. The business-to-business landscape in Memphis is very healthy, and there is a spirit of encouragement among business owners that I haven't experienced in other metropolitan areas. We've discovered that Memphis businesses want other local businesses to succeed, and they are willing to make introductions and help us develop relationships that will benefit our business and our employees."

Jean Shepard: "I am one of those people who was born and raised in Memphis. I grew up around Cooper & Young, going to the Fairgrounds, the MidSouth Fair and the Zoo. When my employer transferred me to such place as Nashville, Richmond, VA, Jackson, MS and Atlanta, GA, I always told everyone that I would always return to my roots in the Memphis area. When I have family or friends visit, we start off with BBQ and then I take them to visit our fantastic Zoo, see the Ducks at the Peabody, walk down Beale

Street and go to Graceland. We have the FedEx Forum, Redbird Stadium, the Pink Palace, Dixon Galleries and the Brooks Museum and many other attractions that can't be beat anywhere. One of the greatest attractions we have is St. Jude's Children's Research Hospital. A few years ago I organized a group of visitors and took them on a tour of the hospital and it was one of the most rewarding experiences of my life."

Don Batchelor: "Memphis Rocks for so many reasons that it is hard to put into words. In short, Memphis has a hometown vibe. Sometimes that vibe is funky... Al Green, Sam and Dave, Booker T and the MGs, the Memphis Horns, Isaac Hayes, Justin Timberlake. Sometimes that vibe is more sophisticated... The Dixon Gallery and Gardens, Opera Memphis, the Brooks Museum, Ballet Memphis, the Memphis Symphony. Sometimes it is more like the Blues... Beale Street, world famous Bar-b-q, the National Civil Rights Museum.

That vibe can also be incredibly creative... innovative charter schools like Soulsville Academy, Holiday Inns, and AutoZone were all founded here. Industries were started here... Piggly Wiggly, the first self-service grocery store; FedEx, the first overnight package delivery service. The vibe can also be the Gospel... many healthy churches doing very innovative work to serve the poor and outcast, just like Jesus did.

And of course, Elvis is the embodiment of all of this in one incredible innovator... soul, gospel, pop, rock, the blues. So I guess I just like my hometown vibe... in all of its beautiful expressions!"

Chapter 16

WHY MEMPHIS ROCKS, ACCORDING TO MEMPHIANS, PART III

This was one of my favorite reader-response series, asking the question, "Why do you think Memphis Rocks?" It was a pleasure sharing some of these responses with readers of the column and now you, as you read this book, because I think the diversity of answers helps capture the true essence and beauty of our community. Let us now wrap up the series with a few more responses from those who live, work and play in this great city of Memphis.

Ann Gilbert: "I think Memphis Rocks because of its wonderful people. Having just moved to the area I can attest to the hospitality, kindness, generosity and caring of the people! The beautiful scenery and soulful nature of the city create a vibrant feel that is rare among larger cities. The increase of business activity and availability of entertainment will help Memphis be recognized as the world class city she is."

Jessie Biggs: "I think Memphis Rocks because you get the best of both city and country life. It is an amazing city with a small town feel where music echoes throughout and good old southern cooking fills the air. You can dance your blues away on Beale Street or run down the banks of the Mighty Mississippi like Huck Finn. Memphis is home for many but it makes an impact on all that pass through."

Erika Adair: "I'm a native Memphian and no matter how many times I move away, I always find myself moving back. Memphis represents: finger licking good BBQ, music, culture, heritage, giving back and paying it forward. All of these things are what Memphis means but most important to me: home sweet home."

Anita Hollis: "Memphis Rocks because even if you are not from the south, everyone makes you feel welcome. Who would not want to live here? You have great food, great venues and a great place to raise your family. My husband and I were both born and raised in Memphis and we love supporting our Memphis TIGERS!! My husband says, "Once a Tiger fan, always a Tiger fan — Never a fair weather fan!" We love supporting all our sports in Memphis because that is what we grew up doing. From the U of M Tigers to the Grizzles to the Redbirds; and no matter which one you go to, you can always get some of that great tasting "Rendezvous BBQ!"

Carla Denton: "Memphis rocks because it floats 'high up on a ridge, just a half a mile from the Mississippi Bridge' (Chuck Berry) and because 'That's where the people smile, smile on you all the while. Hospitality, they were good to me. I couldn't spend a dime, and had the grandest time.' (W C Handy)"

Now, after reading so many touching testimonials, I encourage you to think about what this city and its people mean to you. Then, make it a point to share your thoughts and special moments with others, so that our days will be filled with positives that will both push our city to even greater heights and bring smiles to the faces of those we know and love.

NONPROFIT THEMED

Chapter 17

MEMPHIS GRIZZLIES TEAM UP

Mentoring, like parenting, is critical to the strength of our community. It has been proven that youth with mentors have better grades, decreases in risky behaviors, and improved attitudes toward school and their futures. If we are going to have a safe, vibrant city with a skilled future workforce, each of us must play a part in helping youth build a strong foundation for their life.

Recently, I sat down with the Memphis Grizzlies Charitable Foundation, which was honored in 2012 with the prestigious 'Sport Team of the Year' Award at the Beyond Sport Summit, to learn more about the work they are doing in our community. Established in 2004, the Foundation is committed to serving Memphis youth through mentoring and education, fostering partnerships and providing valuable resources. Since 2001, more than $30 million has been donated to Memphis area nonprofits serving youth. Tens of thousands of children and families have directly benefited from these funds, resulting in new facilities and programs.

We have the unique opportunity of leveraging the popularity of an NBA brand to connect good people with impactful programs. To achieve a 'Greater Memphis', the Grizzlies Foundation will continue to do its part in supporting youth development through mentoring and education. Being a non-native Memphian, it's the ultimate honor to serve this community with Grizzlies TEAM UP.

Joel Katz, Memphis Grizzlies Charitable Foundation

Beyond the financial contributions, the Grizzlies Foundation is working with hands-on involvement and has a number of major undertakings. Two that I think are paramount are the Grizzlies TEAM UP Youth Mentoring Initiative and the Grizzlies TEAM Mentoring Program. Their TEAM UP Youth Mentoring Initiative is a comprehensive community-wide campaign that is building a strong network among mentors in Memphis through active recruitment and recognition, training and program development, advocacy, and placement.

TEAM Mentoring is a relatively new program that implements a group or "team" mentoring program with a 3:9 adult to student ratio. It is an exciting step forward in my opinion because it opens the door to a collaborative mentoring experience both for the youth and adults. The program is currently aimed at middle school aged children with a three semester duration and weekly meetings of about 1 ½ hours per visit.

Group mentoring lowers the level of intimacy and commitment needed for one-to-one matches and gives you a chance to include friends or co-workers to make it a truly fun "teambuilding" experience. You can give it a social or business spin by signing up solo and using the opportunity to build relationships with other leaders, as well. For youth, it gives them more personal connections and allows them to see how adults socially interact in these types of environments. So, let us team up to give back and mentor youth!

How can you give back? Serving as "coach," under their TEAM UP banner, they work with a number of nonprofits that offer mentoring programs and match prospective mentors with the best fit for their interests and schedule. Then, they manage the process to ensure a fun and rewarding experience. Learn more and fill out a quick survey to find your match at www.grizzliesteamup.org.

Chapter 18

MEMPHIS CHILD ADVOCACY CENTER

The Memphis Child Advocacy Center (CAC) is "helping victims become children again." Their mission is to serve children who are victims of sexual and severe physical abuse through prevention, education, and intervention. The nonprofit is child-focused and provides a safe and warm environment for children and families to receive a number of coordinated services, like counseling. It is a remarkable organization both in the services they provide and their holistic, collaborative approach that incorporates therapists, educators, and interviewers working in conjunction with many other agencies in Shelby County.

As a father, it is tremendously scary to know that an estimated 1 in 3 girls and 1 in 5 boys will be sexually abused before age 18. Also frightening is an estimated 9 out of 10 cases are never reported. According to Tennessee law, **ALL adults must report suspected cases of child abuse and neglect.** Abuse of children occurs in every class, race, religion, and neighborhood. As a community, it is something we need to continually focus on stopping, while helping to heal victims.

The team at the CAC guides over 1,000 victimized children and their families to healing, safety, and justice each year. Our prevention program helps stop child sexual abuse from happening for thousands more. Helping kids reclaim their childhood and have a happy, healthy future is an important investment in our community.

Nancy Williams, Memphis Child Advocacy Center

When it comes to helping efforts of the CAC, there are a number of ways you can easily volunteer with an adjustable schedule. As an Ambassador, promote the CAC through personal networks and help raise awareness for child sexual abuse. Coordinate a seminar with an Education Consultant to provide adult training at your business or community organization. Help with administrative duties, like mailings, data entry, and filings, or projects, like window washing and taking inventory of play rooms.

The CAC keeps a "wish list" online where you can view most needed items. A recent list includes baby wipes, G-rated DVDs, new toy trucks, construction paper, and plastic storage bins. These can be in-kind gifts and make a wonderful focus for office or family collections.

Another amazing collection opportunity lies with "Bearing It Together." Upon entering the CAC, each abused child is able to select a teddy bear of his or her choice. Children are encouraged to take their bear to therapy, court, and wherever else they may need extra comfort.

These bears, which play such an important role, are donated by individuals and groups. So, for a truly memorable experience, I recommend hosting a drive for new, generic, colorful teddy bears. There is something remarkable in knowing that you are helping a child find comfort and regain innocence. For more information about supporting the Memphis Child Advocacy Center, please visit www.memphiscac.org.

Chapter 19

MEMPHIS COLLEGE PREP & SCHOLARSHIPS

I recently sat down with Michael Whaley, founder and school director at Memphis College Preparatory Elementary School. Whaley's school is helping redefine the focus and template for our education system and producing astounding results. For example, 71 percent of their kindergarten scholars enrolled at a below basic literacy level. Within two and a half months, 64 percent then tested at or above grade level in literacy. As Whaley states, "We have one focus: college graduation."

Part of the success at Memphis College Prep comes from their model, based on best practices and proven results from the best charter schools in the nation. It also stems from high expectations and rigorous curriculum, including over three hours of literacy instruction and 80 minutes of math instruction every day, in addition to science, social studies, music, and character education. Their school year is longer at 190 days, versus 180, and their day is extended from 7:45am to 4:00pm, which allows for proper academic instruction and support for ambitious goals.

At Memphis College Prep, we have the incredible opportunity to give back by paving the path from kindergarten to college. By maximizing the potential every child has to be successful in school and life, we can transform our schools, our community, and our city.

Michael Whaley, Memphis College Prep
Elementary School

When it comes to local education, there are a number of amazing success stories, like Memphis College Prep and the Jubilee Schools, which have grown from one kindergarten class of 26 students to eight schools now educating over 1,600 students. The Jubilee Schools educate the children, clothe them, wash their uniforms, and provide breakfast and lunch. These students are excelling academically and outperforming on standardized tests in reading, language, and math.

These are stories we need to champion and cultures of learning we need to cultivate. Approximately 70 percent of the necessary tuition for Memphis College Prep comes from government and foundation support, which means there is a 30 percent gap. As Michael and I were talking, we had a number of great ideas pop up, where companies and individuals could easily help with the effort, such as creating a legacy through a scholarship.

In general, I think one of the most gratifying pay-it-forward gifts is a scholarship. As a company, many, including Lipscomb & Pitts Insurance, set aside dollars each year to support youth scholarships, as well as continuing education among personnel.

How can you give back? Earmarking even a nominal amount each month for a local student can create an amazing personal relationship, where you can watch them grow. It gives you confidence knowing you are helping build a more educated workforce and community. I encourage you to check out Memphis College Prep (www.memphiscollegeprep.org) and the Blue Streak Scholarship Fund (www.bssf.net) to see how your support can change lives.

Chapter 20

MEMPHIS RECOVERY CENTERS

Memphis Recovery Centers (MRC) is a licensed, accredited, nonprofit organization that has been treating those with drug and alcohol addictions in the Mid-South for over 40 years. Their primary goal is to help individuals and their families to begin a life-long process of recovery. MRC has three residential programs, one serving adult men and women, and two programs for teens between the ages of 13-17 years of age. The community-referred Youth Program relies on United Way funding and a substantial federal block grant, which sadly is about to be pulled due to the latest economic cuts. Referrals come from pastors, teachers, parents and others in our community. Their program is unique in that they are one of only a few in the state to offer residential treatment for adolescents. MRC is also only one of four in the state to receive this federal funding.

When talking about keys to making our city a safer and better place to live, work, and raise a family, fighting drug and alcohol addiction lies at the root of many issues. It also plays a part in the creative brain trust and production of our city. Growing up, my father shared many sad stories of top executives who lost their jobs and families, as a result of their addictions. Bottom line: battling drug and alcohol addiction deserves our attention and has far reaching affects personally and professionally for the health of our community.

Memphis Recovery Centers (MRC) has been "giving back" to the Memphis Community for over four decades, by providing quality addiction treatment to individuals and their families. MRC informs and educates the Community on addiction and prevention through speaking engagements at churches, schools and health fairs, as well as being a United Way Partner Agency. MRC impacts important Community issues, such as crime, health care and employment by giving men, women and children the tools to achieve life success through recovery.

Judy Goldberg, Memphis Recovery Centers

Addiction treatment addresses many community issues such as crime, unemployment, healthcare and even the homeless population. According to the Community Alliance for the Homeless, there are approximately 1,800 homeless individuals on the streets of Memphis in one given day. Many of these individuals are struggling with addiction and mental disorders. MRC recently expanded its mission to include treating individuals with co-occurring disorders. This means they have a mental disorder in addition to their addiction such as depression, bi-polar disorder, or other diagnosis.

How can you give back? MRC has many opportunities for the community to become engaged. They have a number of fun, public events where they need volunteers and help on various steering committees, like with their MRC Silent Auction, typically held each April. They also need volunteers for their annual 5k Recovery Run, held the Saturday after Thanksgiving.

I encourage you to visit their website, www.memphisrecovery.com, or Facebook page. Contact Judy Goldberg at jgoldberg@memphisrecovery.com to learn more about volunteer opportunities and how you can help make a difference.

Chapter 21

RONALD MCDONALD HOUSE MEMPHIS

Did you know that Memphis boasts a wonderful organization that provides a "home-away-from-home" for families who are in Memphis while their child is receiving treatment for cancer or another catastrophic illness at St. Jude Children's Research Hospital? The name: Ronald McDonald House Charities of Memphis.

When children are sick, parents know it is important to be together as a family and to be able to focus attention on physically comforting them. Indeed, research has shown that family presence in the hospital helps children cope better and heal faster. Ronald McDonald House Charities of Memphis enables families to do just that - focus on the health of their child by providing a home where families can preserve a sense of normalcy with home-cooked meals, comfortable beds and recreational activities. Just as important, the families find a strong support system and establish friendships with other families facing similar anxieties, hardships and uncertainties.

Since opening in 1991, Ronald McDonald House of Memphis has housed more than 7,700 families from nearly every state and 45 countries. In 2012, that number totaled 816. The average stay of their residents is 24 days and the patient range is from birth to age 19. Their beautiful home, which is strategically located nearby St. Jude Children's Research Hospital, offers 51 hotel-style bedrooms, along with large living rooms with fireplaces, common dining rooms with play areas, kitchen space, laundry rooms, an exercise room, TV lounges, playgrounds, and more. The amazing part is that all families stay completely free of charge!

> *Ronald McDonald House of Memphis has provided thousands of Memphians with the opportunity to provide care, comfort and support to families whose children are being treated for cancer at St. Jude. Ronald McDonald House of Memphis also share resources with other nonprofits including Memphis Food Bank, Habitat for Humanity, Neighborhood Christian Centers and the Memphis Union Mission.*
>
> Caron Byrd, Ronald McDonald House Charities
> of Memphis

Although Ronald McDonald House Charities of Memphis is solely associated with St. Jude Children's Research Hospital and receives generous support from the Hospital and McDonald's owners and operators, the organization is an independent, community supported nonprofit that is independently owned and operated. The cost per family stay is approximately $2,600 and the vast majority of funding comes from individuals, corporations, foundations, and civic groups here in our community. Plus, they rely on over 500 volunteers each year to help cover daily and weekly shifts and provide help during major fundraising events, like their annual Radiothon at the end of October and the Big Scoop Ice Cream Festival.

How you can give back: There are many ways to help their efforts. Learn more by visiting www.rmhc-memphis.org or reaching out to their Executive Director, Caron Byrd, at caron@rmhc-memphis.org. Consider taking a tour of the house or pulling together family or co-workers to cook dinner for the families. Encourage others to save pop tabs and donate them during their Pop-Tab-Palooza each fall.

Chapter 22

SAMARITAN'S FEET

Over the last three years the Lipscomb Pitts Breakfast Club has teamed with the Memphis Grizzlies and their charitable foundation to kick off the New Year by hosting a Samaritan's Feet Shoe Distribution. The event has become the launch pad for a National Day of Service, which commemorates the legacy of Dr. Martin Luther King, Jr., who dreamed of people of diverse backgrounds coming together to help those in need. It is fitting that Memphis tips off this 20-city unified effort of community service tied to MLK Day.

This year in Memphis over 100 volunteers from different backgrounds joined us in the Grand Lobby of the FedEx Forum as we washed the feet of more than 300 youth, providing them with new socks and shoes. Volunteers that day were corporate leaders and business owners, U.S. Navy Sailors, Memphis Grizzlies players, educators, government officials, and nonprofit workers. Each year it is inspiring to see so many people coming together, demonstrating such an act of servant leadership and compassion.

Samaritan's Feet believes that it is the HUMAN RIGHT of every child in the world to have a pair of shoes, in order to live DISEASE-FREE from SOIL-TRANSMITTED PARASITES or be PREVENTED from going to SCHOOL. Samaritan's Feet is well on its way to accomplishing its vision of providing 10 million children with 10 million pairs of shoes with a message of hope around the world

Manny Ohonme, Samaritan's Feet

Around the world, nearly 300 million people go without shoes each day and millions are plagued with foot-borne illnesses that may be preventable by simple protection — shoes. This reality is not just confined to third world countries. We have many kids here in Memphis that do not have shoes or are wearing shoes two to three sizes too small for their growing feet. More than the blessing of a new pair of shoes, though, the Samaritan's Feet event offers an opportunity to share a message of hope, compassion, and love. Volunteers symbolically wash the kids' feet, talk and play with them, and let them know we care about their future. Many children walk away saying it was the best day of their life — and volunteers say the same!

I am always moved when Manny Ohonme, founder of Samaritan's Feet, comes to Memphis to share his personal story. Growing up in Nigeria, a missionary gave him his first pair of shoes at age 9. Those shoes allowed him to learn to play basketball, which ultimately earned him a college scholarship and a corporate career. In 2003, he started Samaritan's Feet and his organization has since blessed more than 5 million children and people in need in over 70 countries while engaging over 80,000 volunteers.

Visit www.samaritansfeet.org to learn more about how you can get involved.

Chapter 23

VISIBLE MUSIC COLLEGE

Having worked in the music business out in Los Angeles, I can speak from experience that there is a large gap between having a dream, having the skill set, and having the business acumen to succeed. One of the toughest learning curves for most musicians (or really any creative professional) is embracing the fact that the music business is indeed a "business." When it comes to formal training, the gap seems to widen because most schools tend to focus on theory and skills with little recognition of enterprise and entrepreneurialism. With such a rich legacy in the music industry, it is only fitting that a college breaking the mold would be based here in Memphis.

Visible Music College was founded in 2000 by Ken Steorts, who is a guitarist and one of the original members of the Christian rock band, Skillet. While receiving his college education and traveling on the road with his band, he noticed the gap and decided to act. What he has built over the last thirteen years is truly impressive.

Visible Music College brings top music students from 50 states and 15 countries, to the birthplace of American music — Memphis. With a solid spiritual and professional foundation, we acclimate these students to love the city, serve the people, create new works, and join the raw, ener-getic flow of decades of great Memphis music at events and churches.

Ken Steorts, Visible Music College

Visible Music College ties in the three major categories of Music Production, Music Business, and Modern Music, which encompasses worship leadership, songwriting, vocals, guitar, bass, keyboard, and percussion. The school offers a 3-year accredited bachelor degree program for 125+ students per year. Approximately 450 students have been served thus far, but an even greater metric is that 88 percent of the students are from outside of Memphis and 55 percent remain in Memphis after graduation. So, in its own way, Visible Music College is becoming a wonderful asset for Memphis to recruit and retain some of the best and brightest musical talent from around the world.

In keeping with the theme of "Giving Back," I appreciate that Visible encourages students to become engaged in Memphis. You will find them around town performing in churches and various venues, as well as pitching in with over 4,000 hours of community service.

How can you give back? There are many ways to help their efforts. Take a tour of their beautiful facility at 200 Madison or catch one of their concerts. Hire students for local performances and corporate events. Purchase their Christmas CD, which is definitely a great gift idea for the future. Visit www.visible.edu or contact Ken Steorts at ken@visible.edu for more information.

Chapter 24

UNIVERSITY OF MEMPHIS LEAD

Everyone knows of the University of Memphis blue. What you might not understand, though, is the talent we have in our own backyard. The University of Memphis is developing well-educated, integrity-focused, civic-minded future leaders. As a city, our priority should be to retain and help polish these youth, who quickly will become decision makers and social catalysts.

I can personally speak to the impact of three UofM programs: LEAD, MILE, and Academic Internships. Each is focused on teaming with our community to educate, develop, and retain student leaders by offering an array of co-curricular experiences that equip them for a world of increasing complexity, diversity, and interdependence. While each is different in scope, all provide your company an opportunity to cultivate and leverage top talent.

The Leadership Education and Development program (LEAD) is a holistic leadership platform that includes a four-year academic scholarship complete with classroom instruction, workshops, community projects, mentorships, and active engagement in campus and community organizations. Leadership with accountability is woven into every element of the student's on-campus and off-campus life. The program crosses all majors.

The University of Memphis LEAD program gives back in two ways. First, we are educating, training and developing

*young professionals to stay and help grow the Mid-South
area. Second, we are engaging students in asset based community service projects. We want students to understand
how they can give back and learn of the infinite Memphis
resources and opportunities to make that a reality.*

Dr. Justin Lawhead, University of Memphis

Just through LEAD, the University is investing over $1 million
in scholarship funds annually in leadership development and attracting students from Alaska to Maryland. Spend a minute with a LEAD
student and you will realize the potential impact he or she might have
on your business or our community. There are number of opportunities
to engage with LEAD, like the Professional Connection Lunches, where
you and other business leaders can interact and help groom students in
a fun, moderated discussion centered on leadership. Connect with Dr.
Justin Lawhead (jtlawhed@memphis.edu) to learn more about LEAD.

The Memphis Institute for Leadership Education (MILE) is
a mentorship-based leadership program that pairs top students in
the Fogelman College of Business & Economics with business leaders. The program is geared around an academic year and typically
includes juniors and seniors. These are the cream of the crop, so
MILE provides a tremendous opportunity to interact prior to graduation. As a mentor, you will benefit greatly through the relational
and personal growth dynamics, speakers, and curriculum that
includes everything from ethics to management. Connect with Dr.
Bob Taylor (rrtaylor@memphis.edu) to learn more about MILE.

When it comes to direct results, work with Kathy Tuberville
(ktbrvlle@memphis.edu) and hire an academic intern. The process
is easy, the talent pool is tremendous, and your business will reap
the reward of both training a future leader and having them help
you with immediate business projects. We have had quite a few

interns from the University of Memphis, including Charli Sanders and Alton Cryer, who both worked in our Communications Department. Safe to say, both are headed for greatness! Charli recently graduated and is now doing amazing things with a local nonprofit. Alton will be graduating soon. It has been fun and rewarding watching them grow, but both also brought impressive value to Lipscomb & Pitts Insurance. I highly recommend that you and your company reach out and explore the opportunity of an internship.

Chapter 25

BIG BROTHERS BIG SISTERS OF GREATER MEMPHIS

Did you know that January is known as National Mentoring Month? In Memphis, there is an organization that takes on this charge not just for one month, but for every day of the year. Big Brother Big Sisters of Greater Memphis works to help children reach their potential through professionally supported one-to-one relationships with mentors that have a measurable impact on youth. It is a broad vision reached through the hands of people throughout Memphis.

For more than 100 years, Big Brothers Big Sisters has operated under the belief that inherent in every child is the ability to succeed and thrive in life. As the nation's largest donor and volunteer supported mentoring network, the organization makes meaningful, monitored matches between adult volunteers ("Bigs") and children ("Littles"), ages 6 through 18, in communities across the country. Locally, Big Brothers Big Sisters of Greater Memphis has been serving our community since 1968.

The nonprofit focuses on two types of mentoring programs: Community-based Mentoring and School/Site-based mentoring. With Community-based Mentoring, adults volunteer three to four hours at least twice per month with a youth, for a commitment of at least a year. The two typically get together on their own to spend time developing a one-to-one relationship. With School/Site-based

Mentoring, Bigs and Littles meet once a week for a designated time at a set location, like an elementary school. They engage in recreational and educational activities, as well as school work.

> *Big Brothers Big Sisters makes a difference One Child at a time. Over the last 45 years our volunteers (Bigs) have served over 70,000 children as mentors throughout the Greater Memphis area. We provide our children with strong, enduring and professionally supported one-to-one relationships that change their lives for the better, forever.*
>
> Adrienne Bailey, Big Brothers Big Sisters
> of Greater Memphis

One of their specialty programs is "Amachi," which pairs children of incarcerated parents with mentors. This program has proven to be successful in helping to break the destructive cycle of youth following in their parents' footsteps. Quoting one of my favorite local leaders, "You cannot be what you cannot see." Having a mentor, who can offer unconditional love and show these youth new environments and opportunities, can make all the difference in the world. Just think of the exponential effects for our city if we can steer them toward a life of positive achievement.

The sad part is that federal funding for the "Amachi" program was cut, so Big Brothers Big Sisters is absorbing over $350,000 to keep it active. The good news is that there are many ways we can help their efforts.

How can you give back? Consider being a Big by volunteering just a few hours a month with a child. Donate used cell phones to their recycling program. Give a donation that will help impact a young child's life. Or attend their annual events, like the black-tie and tennis shoes SportsBall. For more information, or to get involved, visit www.msmentor.org.

Chapter 26

MILLION CALORIE REDUCTION MATCH

Healthy Memphis Common Table is a regional health and healthcare improvement collaborative for the Greater Memphis area. The organization is comprised of over 200 community partners and focused on improving the quality of primary care; empowering patients and caregivers; fighting childhood and family obesity; reducing diabetes, heart disease, and pediatric asthma; and eliminating food deserts in low income neighborhoods. They are working at all levels within the healthcare industry, like analyzing data to reduce inefficiencies while working on much larger, broader campaigns that support healthy eating and physical activity.

One such community-wide campaign is the Million Calorie Reduction Match (MCRM). Aimed at reducing obesity rates in Shelby County and improving the nutrition habits and physical activity of citizens, the project seeks to transform the food, beverage, and physical activity environments within corporations, organizations, and community venues through policy change. It is no secret that if we reduce the number of calories we consume and increase our physical activity, we can become healthier. So, the idea is simple, yet powerful: work with employers and stakeholders to create an environment that reduces calories and fosters healthy lifestyle choices and activities.

Just looking around the office, there are simple things that employers can do to reduce available calories and create a more health-conscience environment. Simple things like serving healthier meals and beverages at meetings, providing healthier options in vending machines, and increasing physical activity opportunities, like walking meetings or walk breaks, can make a big difference. Just swapping candy bars with 100 calorie snack options, for example, can yield a calorie reduction of more than a hundred thousand each year. The key is to make the healthy choice the easy choice for your team by focusing on three policies: 1) Healthy meetings/events, 2) Healthy vending, and 3) Healthy physical activity.

Million Calorie Reduction Match is designed to help employers, businesses, municipalities, nonprofits, schools, faith-based and civic organizations develop, adopt, and implement these policies and a reward system for a healthier environment. 2013 was the inaugural year and over 30 organizations that include the City of Memphis and Shelby County governments, Leadership Memphis, the Memphis Grizzlies, Shelby County Health Department, Baptist Hospital, Games Workshop, Methodist Healthcare, Saint Francis Hospital, YMCA, Memphis and Shelby County Airport Authority, Church Health Center, CIGNA, Porter-Leath and Seedco are participating. Healthy Memphis Common Table staff assists participants with the planning, adoption, and assessments. They also connect participants with local resources, as needed. Participants will be recognized for their efforts with Certificates of Achievement.

Learn more about Healthy Memphis Common Table and their Million Calorie Reduction Match at www.healthymemphis.org or contact them directly at 901-684-6011.

Chapter 27

BRIDGES

For over 90 years, BRIDGES has been focused on building personal bridges here in our community by bringing youth and adults from diverse backgrounds together to experience learning that is adventurous, relational, and transformative. Their programs are designed to help students discover personal greatness by igniting motivation and self-confidence, developing their creativity and communication skills, and enhancing their ability to make ethical decisions. The learning also focuses on working effectively as a team, practicing leadership and youth-led social change, as well as initiating and leading complex responses to issues that affect their lives and improve the well-being of the whole community.

With an indoor rock climbing wall and ropes challenge course high overhead, tying "adventurous" into the programs is easy at their futuristic BRIDGES Center. Inclusion and respect for diversity are at the heart of the "relational" experience with strong friendships forged among children from vastly different backgrounds. "Transformative" describes the results of their Bridge Builders programs, which offer youth in grades 6 through 12, three different ways to engage — Connect, Collaborate, and Change. For adults, Team BRIDGES, offers unique team building experiences to corporations and affinity groups.

Through the Bridge Builders program, youth across socio-economic divides come together and learn to appreciate diversity, develop their leadership skills and understand how to make systemic change in the community. By 2020, 60,000 youth will have been through the program. In a city that is still largely segregated and that can benefit from listening to our youth, that is a tremendous gift.

Cynthia Ham, BRIDGES

The proven benefits for students who participate in these programs range from improved academic achievement to increased concern for the welfare of others and the increased belief that one can make a difference in their community. When you think about what that means for the future of Memphis, it is exciting! The organization currently serves more than 12,000 youth and adults annually, who are learning, leading, and helping to lift up our community. Students represent 85 area middle schools and 56 high schools, covering the spectrum of public, charter, parochial, private, and home schooled. BRIDGES is serving all races, religions, and income levels, and truly helping to chart a new course for the interpersonal dynamics of our city.

Getting engaged with BRIDGES is easy. Look at setting up a team-building session, using their rock wall, ropes course, or other experiential learning programs. Take a tour or consider hosting your next party or event at their BRIDGES Center. Learn more by visiting www.bridgesusa.org or reaching out to Melissa Wolowicz at 901-260-3760 or mwolowicz@bridgesusa.org.

Chapter 28

DOROTHY DAY HOUSE OF HOSPITALITY

Sister Maureen Griner was one of the founders of the Dorothy Day House of Hospitality (DDHH) which provides free, temporary housing to homeless families and the means to re-establish their independence. To hear her tell it, the ministry started with faith. "The Dorothy Day House of Hospitality was started with prayer," Sister Griner told me. Back in 2002, prayer led to an appreciation for the efforts of Dorothy Day, who in the early 1930's founded the Catholic Worker Movement with Peter Maurin. The volunteer-based organization served the poor and homeless and opened houses of hospitality to offer support. The DDHH in Memphis, which opened in 2006, is an updated approach to dealing with the needs and realities of homeless families in our community.

Centrally located at 1429 Poplar Ave, the DDHH is just that... a beautiful old house. It is walking distance to grocery stores and schools and has no signage out front. In reality, this house is a blessing and a much needed "pause" in life for families going through hardship and homelessness. The House provides families with basic necessities and safe shelter. And, with assistance from volunteers, the ministry team helps these families identify causes of their homelessness, mentors them, and sets achievable goals to move toward self-sufficiency.

Many people are giving back through their association with the Dorothy Day House of Hospitality. Board members, staff, ministry team and volunteers give our homeless families acceptance, self-esteem and hope for a better future. At the same time, they give the local community an awareness that there are many people in need, and there are many ways each one of us can make a difference.

Sister Maureen Griner, Dorothy Day House
of Hospitality

Sister Maureen and her team already have a number of heartfelt success stories, like helping a young mother graduate college and now live on her own, employed and finishing her MA. Part of their success stems from their focus and innovative template, which is scalable. One of their primary focuses is on situational homelessness, arising when families living paycheck to paycheck suffer a loss of job, car wreck, or house fire.

By providing a free "pause" in life and a chance to save money with a support network in place, they afford families an opportunity to get back on their feet again. Because the DDHH is funded solely through donations from individuals and charitable organizations and comprised of volunteers, they are able to keep overhead costs low and treat each family as a unique entity. They are also able to keep the entire family together, which is uncommon with other agencies.

How can you give back? There are many easy ways to help their efforts. Consider donating household items, like paper towels, light bulbs, laundry supplies, or liquid hand soap. They also need help with general upkeep, like lawn maintenance. You may volunteer your services to help families through mentoring or simply serve a dinner.

Learn more by visiting www.dorothydaymemphis.org or calling Sister Maureen at 901-726-6760.

Chapter 29

MEMPHIS YOUNG LIFE

young Life is truly about relationships and the power of presence in a kid's life. It starts with adults who reach out to youth, on their turf and in their culture, to build bridges of authentic friendship. Young Life leaders spend countless hours with these kids — where they are, as they are — listening and learning what is important to them. Over time, a friendship evolves and youth are strengthened with love and shown that their lives have great worth and purpose. Young Life is also tightening our community fabric by bringing together youth from various high schools, public and private, and fostering compassion and mutual understanding.

Since 1943, Memphis Young Life has been helping teens across the city of Memphis by having caring adults enter into the world of teenagers and offer them authentic friendships that will support them in some of the hardest years of their life. Our hope is that in a few years, some of the same students that were in our program will come back and serve the same under-resourced communities in which they came from. Our goal is to have an impact that can last generations in the city of Memphis.

Jonathan Torres, Memphis Young Life

GIVING BACK WITH PURPOSE

The work Memphis Urban Young Life is doing in our community is hard and necessary. Jonathan Torres, Area Director for Memphis Young Life, actually opened up his house in order to serve more youth at a nearby high school. His wife, likewise, befriended a group of females and has started teaching parenting and other classes that the young women need. The reality is that these kids, which may at first appear hard to love, actually need it most — and Young Life is making a dramatic difference in their lives.

How can you give back? Here are some fun ways you can partner with Young Life:

- Food — Every week they have a "party with a purpose." They are always in need of food/snacks/drinks to provide kids. Anything from pizza to steak can be served. They just want to make sure kids never go home hungry.

- Mock Job Interviews — They are looking for business professionals to help students through mock interviews and help with resumes.

- Corporate Tours — They would love to provide students a chance to tour a business or facility and learn how it operates. By exposing students to various businesses and industries, they can see ahead of high school graduation.

Learn more by contacting Jonathan Torres at 901-726-0054 or torres.younglife@gmail.com.

Chapter 30

PORTER-LEATH

F ounded as an orphanage in 1850, Porter-Leath began as a place where widows and orphans could find food, shelter, clothing, and care. Led by Sarah Leath, a widow and mother herself, the organization was passionately committed to serving at-risk children and families in Memphis. While both its name and mission have evolved over the last 163 years, that same commitment and passion for serving Memphis' most vulnerable citizens lives on today. Porter-Leath currently helps more than 10,000 low-income children and families annually with programs designed to meet their developmental, health, and social needs at the earliest opportunity.

> *Porter-Leath empowers Memphis children and families to achieve a healthy, optimal and independent lifestyle. This venerable 163-year-old nonprofit serves over 10,000 children and families each year.*
>
> Mike Warr, Porter-Leath

The nonprofit has six key programs. "Head Start" offers high quality preschool education to more than 500 of the highest risk children in Shelby County. "Connections" brings nearly 400 children together with families and caregivers in a stable, nurturing environment. "Cornerstone" meets the needs of 600 pregnant and parenting families in their homes. "CareerPlace" provides more than 3,000 parents with skills training and meaningful work experiences. "Generations" provides low-income seniors an opportunity to impact more than 6,500 disadvantaged youth. Then, "Spoonfuls" provides nutritious meals and snacks to more than 800 children each day in 75 family day homes that serve low-income communities.

How can you give back? The best way to learn more about Porter-Leath is to tour their beautiful, historic campus. One smile on the face of a young child in their "Head Start" program will quickly reveal their powerful impact. If you are looking for a fun opportunity to give back to Porter-Leath while enjoying time with friends and family, make plans to attend their Annual City Auto Rajun Cajun Crawfish Festival. The event features free admission, more than 15,000 pounds of crawfish with a variety of vendors selling food, drinks, art, and more (cash only event). There is always great live music and a variety of contests, like crawfish races and crawfish bobbing. My personal favorite is the Gumbo Cookoff. There is nothing like good gumbo for a good cause.

To learn more visit www.porterleath.org or contact Mike Warr at mwarr@porterleath.org.

Chapter 31

FIRST TEE OF MEMPHIS

Founded in 1991 by Charles Hudson, the First Tee of Memphis uses golf as a catalyst for character and life-skills building, as well as providing an outlet for inner-city youth to learn and enjoy the sport, regardless of their financial situation. The organization works with youth ages 5 to 18 from all over the Mid-South and has become recognized as one of the most diverse nonprofits from both a racial and economic perspective. Over 290 kids participate locally each year in their programs and, so far, more than 4.7 million youth have participated in the First Tee programs nationally through 750 program locations.

Located at 974 Firestone Avenue, at the site of the old Firestone tire plant near Downtown, the First Tee of Memphis is revitalizing 92 acres and slowly turning it into an 18-hole golf course. They already have a 450-yard driving range with multiple chipping and putting greens that will soon be open to the public. Their facility provides a positive, safe place for youth, who are surrounded by caring adults in structured environment. Programs take place after-school, on weekends, and during the summer and the cost per child is only $55 for a nine-week session with many children receiving partial or full scholarships.

First Tee of Memphis takes our program to schools, churches and other non-profits, to introduce youth from all over Shelby County to our life skills and the game of golf. First Tee of Memphis gives students and young people honesty, integrity, confidence, responsibility, sportsmanship, perseverance, judgment, courtesy and respect that will prepare them for life.

Nyrone Hawkins, First Tee of Memphis

The key to success is that the First Tee of Memphis is first and foremost a life-skills organization. The focus is on teaching youth skills that allow them to face challenges at home, school, and play in a constructive manner that includes problem solving, managing time, controlling emotions, working well with others, living a healthy lifestyle, and improving relationships…all seamlessly through golf. Mentorship and access to a life-long sport that is known to open doors in the corporate world become icing on the cake.

As testimony of their impact, they were awarded the 2011 *Golf Digest* Award for the Best Municipality in the Country. Another neat success is helping Manassas High School create a golf team, then coach them to 2nd place in their division.

How can you give back? Getting engaged with the First Tee of Memphis is fun and easy. Take a tour of their facility or consider serving as a board member, coach, mentor, or volunteer. For more information, visit www.thefirstteememphis.org or contact their Executive Director, Nyrone Hawkins at 901-526-1480 or nhawkins@ thefirstteememphis.org.

Chapter 32

ST. JUDE CHILDREN'S RESEARCH HOSPITAL

More than 50 years ago, a down-on-his-luck entertainer knelt in a church in Detroit, prayed to Saint Jude Thaddeus asking him to "show me my way in life" and promised to build a shrine in his honor. In 1962, that promise was honored when Danny Thomas opened St. Jude Children's Research Hospital˚.

Thomas realized the power of prayer when, after praying to St. Jude, his career began to flourish. At the height of his career, his TV series, "Make Room for Daddy," brought him worldwide fame. And as his success grew, Thomas began thinking of ways to fulfill his promise to St. Jude. The idea to build a hospital for needy children began to take shape. In 1955, a group of businessmen in Memphis, Tenn., agreed to help support his dream of creating a unique research hospital devoted to curing deadly childhood diseases. More than just a treatment facility, this would be a research center for the children of the world.

St. Jude Children's Research Hospital is leading the way the world understands, treats and defeats childhood cancer and other deadly diseases. St. Jude freely shares the breakthroughs we make, and every child saved at St. Jude means doctors and scientists worldwide can use that knowledge to save thousands more children.

Families never receive a bill from St. Jude for treatment, travel, housing and food — because all a family should worry about is helping their child live.

St. Jude Children's Research Hospital

True to Thomas' word, today St. Jude is leading the way the world understands, treats and defeats childhood cancer and other deadly diseases. Since the hospital opened its doors in 1962, treatments invented at St. Jude have helped push the overall childhood cancer survival rate from 20 percent to more than 80 percent. In 1962, the survival rate for acute lymphoblastic leukemia (ALL), the most common form of childhood cancer, was 4 percent. Today, St. Jude has increased the survival rate for ALL to 94 percent. And St. Jude is working to drive the overall survival rate for childhood cancer to 90 percent in the next day. St. Jude won't stop until no child dies from cancer.

Because the majority of St. Jude funding comes from individual contributors, St. Jude has the freedom to focus on what matters most—saving kids regardless of their financial situation. Families never receive a bill from St. Jude for treatment, travel, housing and food—because all a family should worry about is helping their child live. St. Jude has treated children from all 50 states and from around the world. And since St. Jude freely shares the breakthroughs it makes, every child saved at St. Jude means doctors and scientists worldwide can use that knowledge to save thousands more children.

It costs $1.9 million a day to operate St. Jude, and public contributions provide 75 percent of funding. The average personal contribution is around $30, so it is extremely easy to play a part in saving the lives of precious children. But the most important reason to support St. Jude can be found in the words of St. Jude founder Danny Thomas: "No child should die in the dawn of life."

There are many ways to join the St. Jude mission. Learn more at www.stjude.org.

Chapter 33

SALVATION ARMY MEMPHIS

The Salvation Army began in London in 1865. Evangelist William Booth started a crusade to spread the gospel of Jesus Christ to the poor, the homeless, the hungry, and the destitute by going into the streets and ministering directly to the people. In 1879, The Salvation Army came to the United States and the movement gained momentum throughout the country. Globally, the organization now provides services in over 126 countries.

The Salvation Army in Memphis was established in 1900 by five local churches — First Presbyterian, Second Presbyterian, First Congregational Church, First Methodist and Central Baptist — that each provided start-up funding.

Each day, they provide shelter for about 250 men, women, and children as well as rehabilitation services for women and men. In terms of local impact, last year The Salvation Army in Memphis provided 68,973 nights of lodging, served 200,958 meals, and brought Angel Tree magic to 5,300 children and seniors in need.

The Salvation Army has ministered to the heart of the city for over 113 years. We proudly play a key role in Memphis by providing critical services for the homeless and other neighbors in need throughout the year.

Captain Jonathan Rich, Salvation Army

The Salvation Army focuses on three key areas: Relief, Renewal, and Response. Relief includes immediate assistance like disaster recovery with mobile canteens, an Emergency Family Shelter, Single Women's Lodge, Angel Tree, and veterans and hospital visitations. Renewal focuses on long-term growth including Renewal Place, Adult Rehabilitation Center, Family Worship Centers, and Kroc Community Center. Response offers many ways to serve through donating, volunteering, adopting an angel, or supporting special events.

How can you give back? Seasonal programs, like their Red Kettle campaign and Angel Tree are easy and powerful ways to help their efforts, outside of the daily volunteer opportunities. Contact Amy Beth Dudley at 901-260-9120 or amybeth_dudley@uss. salvationarmy.org for more information about volunteering, adopting a Flock of Angels or ringing the bells at locations throughout the city. Learn more about The Salvation Army and how you can help make a difference by visiting www.salvationarmymemphis.org.

Chapter 34

FELLOWSHIP OF CHRISTIAN ATHLETES

The Fellowship of Christian Athletes (FCA), founded in 1954, is the largest interdenominational, school-based, Christian sports ministry in America. Our local chapter, the Memphis Area FCA, has been active since the mid-1970's and serves middle schools, high schools, and colleges throughout Shelby County. They serve males and females of all races and all economic conditions, in both public and private schools, from the outskirts of the county to the inner city. Memphis Area FCA currently works with 59 campuses and, with additional volunteers and resources, has the potential to impact many more of our schools.

FCA works through what they call the Four C's: Campus, Coaches, Camps, and Community. Their "Campus" Ministry includes team ministry, as well as regular student-initiated and student-led meetings that are typically held on-campus. Through the team ministry, adult volunteers serve as mentors for athletes who many times do not have a good family life or proper role models. Just by being there and investing their time, volunteers are able to build relationships that help instill good character traits such as FCA's core values of integrity, serving, teamwork and excellence. Memphis FCA's fastest-growing aspect of Campus ministry is with females, due to a new program called "FCA Virtuous Woman," which was birthed and developed by Alex Hagler and Kristy Makris of Memphis FCA's staff. It involves a gender-specific curriculum, teaching character traits of women in the Bible.

> *Sports provide a great vehicle for adults to invest in the lives of student-athletes and coaches and give back to our community. Our youth need caring role models and FCA has a place for you to help instill positive values such as integrity, serving, teamwork and excellence. There is not a single public school campus in Shelby County where FCA is not welcome.*
>
> Larry Coley, Fellowship of Christian Athletes

Recognizing the tremendous role that "Coaches" play in the lives of youth, FCA offers numerous programs and resources aimed at support and training. These include prayer support, Bible studies, retreats, special events and regular staff visits. "Camps" entail both local and national times of "inspiration and perspiration" that provide athletic training, competition, clinics, top-notch speakers, small-group sessions, leadership training and more. Scholarship support is raised locally to assist deserving students attending national FCA camps.

How can you give back? The last C, "Community," includes special events and partnerships with local churches and individuals who desire to invest in the lives of athletes and coaches. With a dedicated staff of only five, our Memphis Area FCA depends on a large number of volunteers to work with our area campuses. So, becoming a volunteer is a powerful way to help their efforts.

To get involved in the great work happening at FCA, just visit www.memphisfca.org or call 901-683-3399.

Chapter 35

FRIENDS FOR LIFE

F riends For Life Corporation has been serving the Mid-South since 1985. Originally established as the Aid to End AIDS Committee by a group of friends whose loved ones were dying from complications associated with HIV/AIDS, the organization later became known as Friends For Life and merged with a separate nonprofit, Aloysius Home, to significantly expand its services to include permanent supportive housing. Now, as one of the oldest and most comprehensive AIDS service organizations in the southern United States, Friends For Life serves an average of 2,500 individuals affected with HIV/AIDS annually.

When it comes to programs, Friends For Life has a comprehensive, client-centered approach that includes education, housing, food, and healthy life skills, along with a strong support network. Through collaboration with over 25 medical providers, social service agencies, and pharmaceutical companies, the organization coordinates Wellness University, which offers a variety of educational and skills-building programs with an emphasis on learning how to live with HIV/AIDS. Their Nancy Fletcher Food Pantry is the second largest food pantry in the Mid-South, providing up to 16 tons of food per month to over 1,500 persons affected by HIV/AIDS, including 250 children. Permanent supportive housing is provided in an agency-owned apartment building with other housing provided through tenant based rental assistance.

We are delighted to have the good work our organization does featured in this publication. Lipscomb & Pitts is the model of how businesses can affect a community regarding alerting it to social need and then bravely following that up with social activism. Frankly it is courageous for them to demonstrate this level of servant hood leadership in world that is far too often focused on the bottom line.

Kim Daugherty, Friends for Life

With an estimated 10,000 individuals living in the Mid-South affected by HIV/AIDS, there is much that we can do to help further their efforts. Part of their goal is to help heighten awareness, facilitate acceptance, and promote prevention in the community. Many stories are touching and counter to stereotypes, like a young man who was infected through a blood transfusion related to a medical emergency. Friends For Life offers HIV testing, along with prevention education that is extremely valuable for our community, in order to be equipped with facts.

How can you give back? There are many opportunities to volunteer. The organization hosts free congregate meals, known as Feast for Friends, twice a month at St. John's Methodist Church. Consider helping to cook or serve a meal. Help is always appreciated in the food pantry to help re-stock the shelves. Or simply drop by and visit to see what Friends for Life is doing!

Learn more about Friends For Life Corporation by visiting www. friendsforlifecorp.org or contacting their Executive Director, Kim Daugherty, at 901-272-0855 or kim.daughtery@friendsforlifecorp.org.

Chapter 36

MID-SOUTH FOOD BANK

M id-South Food Bank is an independent, nondenominational nonprofit that was founded in 1981 with the vision of creating a hunger-free community. Their programs impact 220,000 individuals in 31 counties in west Tennessee, north Mississippi, and east Arkansas. More than one-third are children and 10 percent are seniors. All of them need food to meet basic nutrition needs, in order to lead healthy, productive lives.

Mid-South Food Bank has four primary hunger fighting programs: Hunger's Hope, Feeding Children, Mobile Pantry, and Disaster Relief. Hunger's Hope distributes food and groceries through a network of 215 agencies with more than 300 feeding programs. These include food pantries, soup kitchens, shelters, youth and senior programs, rehabilitation and residential centers. Last year, these agencies distributed 13 million pounds of food — the equivalent of 11 million meals.

> *Mid-South Food Bank not only gives people food, we are providing the means to take people in need from hunger to health, and that is so important. Thanks to the generous support of the Mid-South community, we are able to help children, families and seniors who face food insecurity and hunger, making every day less of a struggle.*
>
> Estella Greer, Mid-South Food Bank

Feeding Children addresses the nutritional needs of approximately 136,000 children. Last year, for example, 207,000 backpack meals were enjoyed by children who might not otherwise have had a nutritious meal to eat. Mobile Pantry provides truck loads of food for distribution in 20 rural and underserved counties. Mobile Pantry also provides fresh produce to youth and seniors, who live in inner city food deserts. Disaster Relief is offered as a first response to supply emergency shelters with food when disaster strikes.

How can you give back? Helping the efforts of Mid-South Food Bank is easy and critical, as they currently face dire shortages. Coordinate or participate in a food drive with family, friends, or co-workers. Most needed items include canned meats, soups, peanut butter, canned fruits, canned vegetables, canned fruit juice, and any non-perishable items (no glass containers). They have four food collection sites and a brochure online that provides all the details necessary to facilitate your own food drive.

Financial contributions are powerful, as every dollar donated translates to 3 nutritious meals. Take a tour of their facility or consider volunteering. Learn more and help feed those in need by visiting www.midsouthfoodbank.org.

Chapter 37

MIFA

MIFA was founded in September of 1968 by a group of ministers and community members who came together in the turbulent months following Dr. Martin Luther King, Jr.'s assassination. Out of their spirit of cooperation and determination to create positive change, those organizers, who were MIFA's first volunteers, set the stage for an agency that would quickly mature to unite the community through service. Over the last 45 years, MIFA has evolved from advocacy to direct service, from grassroots to a sophisticated professional operation, from a radical effort doomed for failure to a leader in the nonprofit community.

From the beginning, volunteers provided strategic guidance and used MIFA as an incubator to create new programs for the community. Some programs that started at MIFA later spun off and have remained independently successful, like The Mid-South Food Bank, *The Best Times*, and Memphis Child Advocacy Center. Other ideas, like MIFA Transit, Meals on Wheels, and Emergency Services have become mainstays in their current program lineup.

> *MIFA unites the community through service. Our founding philosophy was one of unity, and we remain a place where people of all backgrounds can come together to serve their neighbors.*

Sally Jones Heinz, MIFA

MIFA Transit started in the summer of 1974 with one driver and a borrowed Salvation Army bus. Today, a fleet of 16 vehicles transports seniors to and from medical appointments, senior centers, and on other critical errands.

MIFA Meals on Wheels started in 1976, and its success was contingent upon the availability of volunteers who could deliver meals to far-flung areas in Shelby, Fayette, Tipton, and Lauderdale counties, in addition to the metro area. Today, the program's focus is on Shelby County, and about 80 volunteers deliver meals every weekday. The program served more than 404,000 meals last year.

Emergency Services was established in 1975 to provide essentials, like food and clothing to people in need. Today, it helps individuals and families in crisis with rent, mortgage, and utility payments and provides food vouchers. More than 15,000 people received aid last year.

How can you give back? There are many ways to volunteer and help the efforts of MIFA. Take just one hour to deliver meals or consider a more specialized role, like board member or consultant. Get your hands dirty with MIFA's Hands on Home program, building wheelchair ramps for low-income senior homeowners with no construction experience required. Then, instead of purchasing tickets to a fancy gala, plan on not attending their No-Go Gala and instead enjoy a provided activity with your family.

Learn more by visiting www.mifa.org, and definitely check out their section on Something Good in Memphis.

Chapter 38

OVARIAN CANCER AWARENESS FOUNDATION

E ight years ago, one event spearheaded the formation of an organization that reaches into countless lives throughout the Mid-South on a daily basis. For Linda Vance, her family's world was rocked when her daughter received the diagnosis of "ovarian cancer." At roughly the same time, another family in Memphis received the same news and when they could not find any information or people to talk with, founded the Ovarian Cancer Awareness Foundation.

The organization hosts monthly survivor meetings to share stories and present speakers who share pertinent tips on how to best handle the disease. Volunteers visit local clinics and provide information and "goodie bags" to the families and individuals undergoing chemo treatments. "Goodie bags" contain a warm blanket, ginger ale (the beverage of choice for controlling nausea), paper and pencils to journal or record doctor comments, and other things that may help on their journey. The Ovarian Cancer Awareness Foundation recently joined the "Survivors Teaching Students" program to share their stories with medical students, in order to help them better understand the disease.

We know we are making a difference at the Ovarian Cancer Awareness Foundation when ladies come up to us at an event and tell us the bookmark or flyer they received

saved their life. We continually explain to women they are the only ones that know when something is wrong and it's up to them to push doctors to find the root cause, thus the phrase "It whispers, listen to your body."
Linda Vance, Ovarian Cancer Awareness Foundation

The older I get, sadly the more friends, family, co-workers, and acquaintances that I know who are dramatically impacted by cancer. It seems like just within the last year, we have lost many tremendous leaders and compassionate givers in our community, along with some close friends. When it comes to ovarian cancer, about 27,000 women in the United States will get a diagnosis each year, and about 14,000 will die from the disease. It is the ninth most common cancer among women and ranks fifth in cancer deaths among women, accounting for more deaths than any other cancer of the female reproductive system.

The good news is that if ovarian cancer is found while it is in Stage I or II and is treated before the cancer has spread outside the ovary, the five-year survivor rate is 94 percent. Since diagnosing the disease is difficult and there are no specific screening tools, the key to early detection is heightened awareness and education, including knowledge of risk factors and symptoms. Symptoms include general abdominal pain, bloating, diarrhea, unexplained weight gain, and fatigue. So, the Ovarian Cancer Awareness Foundation's mission is to encourage national awareness about ovarian cancer, promote education about the disease, and also coordinate the programs and activities that offer support for individuals and families impacted, survivors, and caregivers.

Learn more about ovarian cancer and the Ovarian Cancer Awareness Foundation by visiting www.ocafoundation.org.

Chapter 39

GiVE 365

GiVE 365 is simple in premise: give $365 — a dollar a day — to make our community better. Pool those dollars with others to make a collective impact and decide together which organizations will receive the money. The formula is easy to understand and powerful for our community, but there are also three lessons it teaches that are invaluable.

First is "planned" philanthropy. Having a plan is critical to success in every instance of life, whether with your business, family, personal finances, or retirement. We typically hear this advice: "if you fail to plan, you plan to fail." Fred Smith with FedEx famously phrases it with six P's: "Proper Planning Prevents Piss Poor Performance." Either way, this premise holds true with philanthropy, too.

Establishing a plan that sets aside a percentage of your monthly or yearly income for nonprofit giving, like you would for your Church, fosters a foundation and mindset for sustainable impact. Set aside a certain dollar amount per month that can be allocated as a donation or a date night for a nonprofit-related event or treat it like a savings account and make larger contributions at the end of the year. With GiVE 365, the plan is a manageable $1 a day or around $30 a month, which can be allocated monthly or yearly to fit your budget.

The Community Foundation offers donors so many ways to strengthen our community through philanthropy.

From managing donors' private charitable funds to offering opportunities to come together and pool their money with others — like GiVE 365 and the Community Partnership Fund — we give back by empowering donors to make their charitable giving go as far as possible.

Robert Fockler, Community Foundation
of Greater Memphis

Second is "engaged" philanthropy. While financial resources are important, money does not solve problems — people do! It is critical that our leaders, future leaders, and children understand they must lend their time, talents, and effort to help strengthen Memphis. This means being an active citizen who learns about local nonprofits, aligning resources, building capacity, and expanding spheres of influence.

GiVE 365 sets the stage to interact with and learn about nonprofits, review grant proposals and vote on grant awards, and build your sphere of influence by networking with other contributing members. Also, you learn how to gauge impact and track the results of your contributions, which is always exciting.

Third is "collective" philanthropy. Like a drop of water that falls into a pond and creates ripples, the concept of starting small and building momentum to create a tidal wave of impact is powerful. Since 2010, members of GiVE 365 have awarded nearly $225,000 in grants to 27 organizations. The GiVE 365 endowment now totals almost $290,000 and there are more than 320 member households contributing. As the number of GiVErs grows, so too will the collective impact.

Learn more about GiVE 365 by visiting www.cfgm.org.

Chapter 40

tn**ACHIEVES**

tnAchieves evolved from knoxAchieves, which began in 2008 as an economic development initiative out of Knox County Mayor Mike Ragsdale's office. Due to the program's success, it was quickly charged with the task of expanding its program statewide. Aided by the support of Tennessee Governor Bill Haslam, who as Knoxville Mayor, helped lead knoxAchieves since its inception, the program was rebranded as tnAchieves and has grown to include 27 counties.

tnAchieves is a last dollar scholarship and mentoring program designed to provide an opportunity for Tennessee public high school graduates to receive up to $4,000 annually for community or technical college tuition. The scholarship applies for two years or four consecutive semesters and the amount of money awarded is determined after all other sources of scholarships and financial aid have been granted. Often this scholarship is critical in helping students bridge the gap and overcome financial obstacles that might have deterred them otherwise.

> *The foundation of tnAchieves is volunteerism. Our students are required to complete community service hours each semester in an effort to foster a culture of giving back. In essence, the success of tnAchieves stems from the generosity of our communities.*
>
> Krissy DeAlejandro, tnAchieves

GIVING BACK WITH PURPOSE

The tnAchieves model is uniquely volunteer-driven. Volunteer donors from across the state provide the funds for scholarships, so the program is completely privately funded. Volunteers serve as mentors and counselors to the students. Scholarship recipients then volunteer their time by completing at least eight hours of community service each semester.

tnAchieves currently offers its program to nearly 50 percent of the state's public high school seniors. Here in Shelby County, the program has sent nearly 1,200 students to a post-secondary institution in only two years. Two more shining statistics are 70 percent of tnAchieves students are first generation students and the amount of community service hours logged by scholarship recipients tops 10,000. It is easy to see the impact it is having with students, but it comes full circle when you consider this scholarship is helping to supply an educated workforce and foster a culture of giving back.

How can you give back? One of the best ways to help the efforts of tnAchieves is to volunteer as a mentor. The time investment is minimal at only 10-15 hours annually, so it is a perfect opportunity for busy professionals and corporate teams. Each mentor assists five high school seniors, primarily with their enrollment process and form completions. Typical interaction includes reminding them about deadlines, sharing your college experiences, and offering words of encouragement. Many times, it is interacting through text messages and simply letting them know someone cares and is willing to help.

Learn more and apply online at www.tnachieves.org or contact Kaci Murley at kaci@tnachieves.org or 901-258-2177.

Chapter 41

MEMPHIS CRISIS CENTER

F ounded in 1970, the Memphis Crisis Center has grown from the vision of a few caring doctors to a full-service, 24/7 lifeline for those in need of a caring ear or support in times of crisis and distress. Trained volunteers — using a combination of empathetic listening, risk assessment, and crisis intervention — assist callers with immediate issues and link them with the long-term resources they need to cope and overcome them. As a United Way agency and partner with the University of Tennessee Health Science Center, the Memphis Crisis Center's services are free of cost, 100 percent secure, and always totally confidential.

Their 24-hour lifeline, 901-CRISIS-7 (901-274-7477), is the first place our citizens can turn when things seem out of control. Having someone at the other end of the line, who is listening compassionately without judging, while talking through the hurt to find a solution literally helps make the difference between life and death. The MCC received over 17,000 calls last year with approximately 1,200 related to suicide. Typical calls can include a wide range of issues, such as alcohol and drug abuse, domestic violence, depression, sexual assault, relationship issues, bullying, and suicidal thoughts.

The MCC gives back to the community every day 24/7 by offering help, building hope, and saving lives through compassionate volunteer-powered service. Your life is at least worth a phone call.

Mike LaBonte, Memphis Crisis Center

The Memphis Crisis Center also administers the Call4Kids Hotline and partners with Crimestoppers on the SeniorBSafe Line. Both programs can be accessed through 901 CRISIS-7. Call4Kids handles calls where a child or teenager's safety is at-risk. SeniorBSafe is for seniors or others who feel unsafe in their neighborhoods or suspect illegal activity. For those needing information about living with HIV/AIDS, the agency operates 1-877-HIV-KNOW.

They are the local affiliate of the National Suicide Prevention Lifeline (1-800-273-TALK). Along with its crisis services, the Memphis Crisis Center offers free suicide awareness and prevention workshops to community groups and schools.

Personally knowing someone who called the Memphis Crisis Center after losing a loved one and facing overwhelming change in his life, I have seen firsthand the way it can lift Memphians up and give them hope.

How can you give back? Now is the perfect time for us to step up and help by volunteering. They have a full training program for those interested in serving and it is a wonderful opportunity to give back. It is powerful thing to know you helped a senior, protected a child, and saved a life!

Learn more at www.MemphisCrisisCenter.org. Contact volunteers@crisis7.org or 901-649-8572 for volunteer opportunities.

Chapter 42

THE SOULSVILLE FOUNDATION

The Soulsville Foundation was created in Memphis in the late 1990s by a group of concerned local business leaders, philanthropists, and former employees of Stax Records to ensure that the rich legacy of the Soulsville, USA community would not be lost to history. Soulsville was home to Stax in the 1960s and '70s, but, unfortunately, found itself in a state of blight and decay in the decades following. All of that has definitely changed, though! When you step foot on the Soulsville campus now, you see a vibrant future with hundreds of smiling students, modern schools, a world-class museum, and a community embracing its role as a beacon of opportunity.

The Soulsville Foundation funds and operates three subsidiary organizations on its campus: The Soulsville Charter School, Stax Music Academy, and Stax Museum of American Soul Music. Launched in 2005, The Soulsville Charter School is a tuition-free public charter school that combines an academically rigorous core with a music-rich environment to prepare students for success in college. The school serves approximately 500 students in grades six through twelve, operating on a lottery basis and realizing impressive results. ALL 51 seniors in their first graduating class of 2012 were accepted to college with a combined total of more than $3.8 million dollars in scholarships! About 80 percent of those students were the first in their family to attend college.

GIVING BACK WITH PURPOSE

The Soulsville Foundation serves more than 700 young people daily through our Stax Music Academy and The Soulsville Charter School. With our Stax Museum we honor and celebrate all of the Stax Records artists, many of whom had all been forgotten as recently as a dozen years ago.

Mark Wender, The Soulsville Foundation

Stax Music Academy is a unique learning center that serves primarily at-risk youth with mentoring experiences, high-quality music education programs, and performance opportunities. The Stax Museum of American Soul Music, opened in 2003, is the world's first and only full-fledged soul music museum. It has quickly become a worldwide tourist destination and has welcomed hundreds of thousands of people into its 17,000 square feet of exhibits and vast collection of memorabilia, along with live music events, special exhibits, panel discussions, and community outreach programs.

How you can give back? It all starts with learning. Find out more about The Soulsville Foundation by experiencing the magic of the Stax Museum of American Soul Music, taking a tour of the schools, or visiting www.soulsvillefoundation.org.

Chapter 43

FAMILY SAFETY CENTER

The Family Safety Center is a success story for the power of persistence and collaboration. Rather than giving up in 2005 when a federal grant for a family justice center was denied, community leaders, spearheaded by the Memphis Shelby Crime Commission, took it upon themselves to bring the organization to fruition. To create their model, they tapped into the expertise of the Memphis Child Advocacy Center, which utilizes a multi-agency team response to child abuse in Memphis. Together, the group led planning and fundraising efforts and helped bring 23 partner agencies together to serve victims of domestic violence. With their grand opening on April 26, 2012, the Family Safety Center is now a reality, providing hope for victims and healing for families.

Similar to drug or alcohol abuse, sexual abuse, or child abuse, domestic violence affects our entire community. It knows no skin color, income level, or affiliation of faith. Domestic violence is defined as a pattern of controlling behavior that consists of physical, sexual and/or psychological abuse or assaults committed by one intimate partner against another. It often occurs because a partner wants to control the thoughts, beliefs and conduct of his or her significant other. While the violence is usually directed at a particular victim, everyone suffers — children, families, friends, and co-workers.

Hope and healing with dignity and respect are what we strive to give back to victims and their families. As one survivor recently said to me, "The Family Safety Center provides an umbrella during stormy times." We seek to provide that sense of comfort to all victims, their families and our community.

Olliette Murry-Drobot, Family Safety Center

The Family Safety Center provides a safe haven for victims of domestic violence and offers specially trained navigators, who listen and assess immediate and long-term needs, in order to guide victims to the appropriate resources available to help them. The 23 partner agencies are available on and off-site and collaborate to help with civil and criminal services, like assistance with emergency protective orders, legal advice, court advocacy, and prosecution support. The agencies help with health and social services, including safety planning, referrals to confidential emergency shelters, and counseling, along with offering spiritual and chaplain services, as well.

How can you give back? Education and awareness about domestic violence is the key to empowering our citizens to recognize warning signs, realize the danger, report the crime and reach out for help. For this reason, the Family Safety Center provides training to community and corporate groups, which would be a great enrichment opportunity for your team.

In terms of helping their efforts, they have a detailed wish list on their website, including cleaning supplies, children's DVDs, and gift cards. Learn more by visiting www.familysafetycenter.org or calling 901-222-4400.

Chapter 44

SRVS

S RVS was founded on November 1, 1962 by a group of parents who wanted a safe working environment for their loved ones with developmental disabilities. The parents joined together to form SRVS Industries, which was and remains an active, on-site facility where individuals with disabilities are employed, offering services like labeling, hand assembly, packaging, and more. In the 1970's MARC, a nonprofit advocacy agency, started the first group home and a day center for adults. In the 1980's MARC and SRVS Industries merged to form SRVS.

SRVS is the only agency in West Tennessee that provides residential, employment, clinical and learning center services under one roof. The organization also offers elder and adult care. It is impressive to know that no matter how severe the disability, SRVS does not refuse service to anyone. They support more than 800 individuals with disabilities with a dedicated staff of 900 people and an estimated economic impact of $97 million to our community.

Over its 50 year history SRVS has given back to Memphis in many ways, from empowering families to helping build the city's human capital. The services we provide support people with disabilities and enable their families to work and contribute to their communities.

Tyler Hampton, SRVS

SRVS has a beautiful, state of the art new headquarters, located at 3971 Knight Arnold. The new facility affords them the opportunity to double their capacity and serve more families with enhanced programming and services. The main program space is the SRVS Learning Center with weekday programs for adults that concentrate on academic, social skills, self-care skills, and pre-vocational training utilizing Montessori teaching techniques. SRVS is actually the first agency to provide Montessori teaching to adults with disabilities. Some of my favorites are the music room, art room, the model apartment to teach independent living, the teaching kitchen, computer lab, and the sensory stimulation room with curtains of lights and bubble columns that glow. It is definitely worth taking a tour!

How can you give back? There are many ways to help the efforts of SRVS. Volunteering is an important and extremely rewarding opportunity because I guarantee you will receive hugs, high-fives, and tons of smiles. Consider spending an hour socializing with the adults, like banging on the bongo drums, crafting art, reading, or planting in their garden.

Learn more about SRVS, their programs, volunteer opportunities, job postings, and events by visiting www.srvs.org.

Chapter 45

VICTIMS TO VICTORY

Unfortunately, large cities, like Memphis, face the reality of homicides and other crimes of violence. While we have been successful at reducing the violent crime rate over the years, this does not lessen the impact on those families directly affected. For every one person that is murdered, estimates show at least 10 to 12 primary survivors who experience the traumatic impact of grieving the death of a loved one. These survivors include children, adult relatives, significant others, and friends who not only grieve, but may find their lives complicated by stressful investigations, a confusing and lengthy criminal justice process, diminished ability to function at work or school, and unexpected financial costs.

Launched in January 1995, Victims to Victory (VTV) is a Christian nonprofit that responds to the emotional, spiritual, and practical needs of these family members, who have felt the traumatic impact of violent crime. Last year alone, the organization served more than 320 victims. The organization's outreach is primarily directed through referrals from the Memphis Police Department. Most clients are African-American females frequently left to care for children and adolescents who have lost a parent to violent death. Some of these youth are at risk because of having witnessed or been exposed to violence.

Victims to Victory brings skillful, trained, loving profes-
sional assistance to families who are suffering the worst
that can happen. If you read about a murder, chances
are that Victims to Victory staff and volunteers are there
assisting the grieving families. Through counseling, group
meetings, training, resourcing and court accompaniment,
Victims to Victory helps begin the recovery process.

Don Batchelor, Victims to Victory

VTV improves the well-being of crime survivors and assists them in stabilizing their lives by offering practical assistance, emotional help, and spiritual support. Primary services include in-home crisis counseling, youth and adult support groups, court accompaniment and criminal justice advocacy, and assistance in securing victim compensation benefits, like funeral and burial costs. Spiritual support is offered through prayer, faith-based referrals and resources, and special encouragement events, like the Annual Hope and Remembrance Candlelight Service.

How can you give back? There are many ways you can help the efforts of VTV. The organization hosts several events each year, like a 5k Victims Walk and the Hope and Remembrance Candlelight Service each December. Consider participating in these events by helping to promote, volunteer, or recruiting your employer to become a sponsor.

I encourage you to learn more by visiting www.victimsto victory.org or contacting their Executive Director, Dr. Katherine Lawson at 901-274-5012 or klawson550@aol.com.

Chapter 46

AGAPE CHILD & FAMILY SERVICES

Agape Child & Family Services was founded in 1969 with the mission to be a Christ-centered ministry that provides children and families with healthy homes. The word Agape means "love," and in this case, that love is for children, for families, and for Christ. They are dedicated to the premise that every child deserves a stable, loving, and permanent family, so each of their comprehensive programs and services revolves around that core principle. Overall, Agape will serve more than 10,000 children, adults, and families through its services this year.

One of Agape's noteworthy programs aimed at community restoration and transformation is the Powerlines Community Network (PCN). Through the PCN, Agape has been able to create a collaborative network of churches, businesses, volunteers, and other stakeholders that help connect under-resourced neighborhoods with the resources they need to create a more nurturing environment for children and families. Since each neighborhood has different needs, Agape has created a trackable system and process to assess the situation, garner feedback and gauge the needs, then respond in the most appropriate manner.

Agape's cause is 'sharing what we have with those we serve.'
As God has given abilities, finances, position, and resources
to many who serve through Agape, we help equip them

(and ourselves) to share these very gifts with those we are honored to come alongside at Agape...especially youth and families in under-resourced communities.

David Jordan, Agape Child & Family Services

Another impressive Agape program is Families In Transition (FIT). FIT is the only program of its kind in Shelby County serving homeless, pregnant women and their children in transitional housing for up to two years. FIT provides a number of services, like an apartment, life skills classes, counseling, mentoring, and case management assistance, at no cost to the families. They have successfully helped over 150 women and I have personally met a number of their heart-warming success stories, over the last few years.

How can you give back? There are many ways to help the efforts of Agape Child & Family Services. Consider becoming a volunteer or mentor where you can help a child with homework, mentor a youth in foster care, or mentor a mother in their FIT program. Everyday Agape needs at least 40 volunteers for their programs, so there is always an easy opportunity to serve.

Learn more about Agape by visiting www.agapemeanslove.org or calling 901-323-3600.

Chapter 47

CALVARY RESCUE MISSION

Betty and Milton Hatcher first opened the doors of Calvary Rescue Mission on April 1, 1967. Then and now, the organization remains focused on providing temporary shelter, food, and clothing to homeless men in need. They serve two full meals a day, breakfast and dinner, and take pride in the fact that the home-cooked meals with plentiful portions quickly add strength and much needed nutrition to those served. In conjunction with the nightly lodging, food, and clothing, Calvary also provides nightly chapel services, counseling, a discipleship program, and a library of over 2,500 books. Over 529,000 men have been served since Calvary was established.

The dignity, respect, and loving care that men receive at Calvary is unique and a valuable part of the physical and emotional re-building process. Every evening, following a home-cooked meal, area ministers and church leaders conduct Christian worship services. Combined with the counseling from an experienced and dedicated staff, many men at Calvary have had life changing experiences enabling them to overcome drug and alcohol dependency, depression, and other challenging times. They have a number of great success stories, like Sammie Armstead, who grew up in a good family, but made mistakes as a young adult and found himself homeless. Now, Sammie is fully employed, married, and living a productive and fulfilling life. He serves on Calvary's Board of Directors.

Since 1967, Calvary Rescue Mission reaches out to our community at Thanksgiving by providing 400 meals to needy families and individuals. At Christmastime, we provide gift bags for 750 precious children. We are only able to do this by the grace of God and our army of faithful prayer warriors, volunteers, and supporters.

Bob Freudiger, Calvary Rescue Mission

A Calvary van goes downtown every day and transports homeless men to the Mission, located at 960 S. Third. Their facility is a small, converted 1920's era church building that can accommodate 46 men, plus staff. Since estimates place the Memphis homeless population around 1,800, Calvary seeks to expand their outreach, in order to help a larger number and percentage of homeless men with each passing year.

How can you give back? Learn more about Calvary Rescue Mission by visiting www.calvaryrescue.com or calling 901-774-3399. There are many volunteer opportunities at the Mission, along with opportunities to support their efforts at events throughout the year.

Chapter 48

NEW BALLET ENSEMBLE

Some of my most prized memories over the last year are cultural experiences, like sitting on stage while Mei Ann Chen conducted a rehearsal for the Memphis Symphony Orchestra, watching a private performance of "Being Here" with Ballet Memphis, and seeing the Memphis Symphony team with the Dixon Gallery & Gardens for their Symphony in the Gardens. This collaborative atmosphere, where our world-class cultural arts organizations are working together, is unique to Memphis and something we should hold with pride.

New Ballet Ensemble is another example of how Memphis is charting a new course for cultural arts. Established in 2002, the school sprang from founder, Katie Smythe's vision to offer children from various socio-economic and racial backgrounds the benefits of ballet training on the level that was traditionally reserved for those who could afford the best. Their mission is to provide opportunity for all with the core beliefs that children from different backgrounds can and should enrich each other's lives, arts education should address the whole child, all students should dance regardless of their ability to pay, and dance training opens pathways to college.

"New Ballet is grateful to donors such as the Assisi Foundation, Arts Memphis, the Plough Foundation and generous

*individuals who helped us build space so that we could
give back by opening our doors."*

Katie Smythe, New Ballet Ensemble

There are many local organizations or start-ups that have
no access to rehearsal space in a professional facility. New Ballet
Ensemble provides studio and meeting space, and sprung floors for
dance specific projects at negligible rent. The space is free to partners in performance. Hatiloo Theater, Bantaba African, Outloud
Artistry and The Shelby County Links, among others, have all used
the ArtsMemphis-funded Community DanceSpace at New Ballet
Ensemble for dance specific projects. This collaborative spirit allows
these organizations to save their precious funds for other necessary
expenses and is mutually beneficial. DanceSpace partners enhance
and complement the diverse community at New Ballet Ensemble.
Indeed, Memphis artists cherish this space, calling it "home."

By leveraging contributions to underwrite scholarships and
training, New Ballet Ensemble is realizing impressive success. Graduates have attended or are currently attending universities, like NYU
Tisch School of the Arts, Boston Conservatory, the Universities of
Arizona, Georgia, and Oklahoma, all in Dance Majors or Minors.
Graduates have been featured on MTV, "So You Think You Can
Dance," and the TODAY Show to name a few. Their favorite statistic,
though, is that 40% of their student body is from minority groups and
over 38% of their students in the Core program are on scholarships.

Learn more about New Ballet Ensemble by visiting www.new
ballet.org or contacting Katie Smythe at katie@newballet.org or
901-726-9225.

Chapter 49

FACING HISTORY AND OURSELVES

F ounded in Brookline, Massachusetts in 1976 by an educator, who grew up in Memphis, Tennessee, Facing History and Ourselves has grown from an innovative course taught in a single school district to an international organization with more than 150 staff members. Through nine offices in North America, an international hub in London, and educational partnerships that span the globe, the organization reaches more than 29,000 educators and nearly 2 million students per year. Since the Memphis office opened in 1992, Facing History and Ourselves has provided professional development and resources for 2,500 area teachers and impacted over 100,000 middle and high school students in the greater Memphis area.

Facing History's mission is to engage students of diverse backgrounds in an examination of racism, prejudice, and anti-Semitism in order to promote the development of a more humane and informed citizenry. By studying the historical development and lessons of the Holocaust and other examples of genocide, students make the essential connection between history and the moral choices they confront in their own lives. The organization provides resources, seminars, and public events to provide opportunities for people of all ages to recognize the importance of civic participation and to learn from the courage and resilience of others. They even have a semester-long Facing History high school elective course that has been certified by the Tennessee Department of Education.

Facing History provides ideas, methods, and tools that support the practical needs, and spirits, of educators worldwide who share the goal of creating a better, more informed, and more thoughtful society.

Rachel Shankman, Facing History and Ourselves

The organization recently hosted a free public exhibition, Choosing to Participate, at the Benjamin L. Hooks Central Library. Choosing to Participate is part of a global initiative encouraging young people and adults to explore the question, what does it mean to be a citizen in a democracy? The exhibition challenged visitors to recognize that our choices matter — to ourselves, our community, and our world.

Visitors viewed four multimedia installations about people and communities whose stories illustrate how courage, initiative, and compassion are necessary to protect democracy. Exhibits included *Not in Our Town*, which described how citizens in Billings, Montana came together to fight a series of hate crimes, and *Little Things Are Big*, which told the story of a Puerto Rican man who, late one night, encountered a white mother in need of assistance on the New York subway in the 1950s. In both cases, people standing up for what was right — being "upstanders" as opposed to bystanders — made a tremendous impact on the lives of others.

Learn more about Facing History and Ourselves by visiting www.facinghistory.org.

Chapter 50

THE EXCHANGE CLUB FAMILY CENTER

The Exchange Club Family Center is an organization that is focused on breaking the cycle of child abuse and neglect by replacing abusive and violent behavior with effective parenting skills.

Opened in 1984 through the efforts of six local Exchange Clubs, it is one of over 60 Exchange Club Centers across the nation. With the help of 35 experienced staff members and 150 community volunteers, the agency served over 5,500 children and adults here in the Mid-South last year. They offer 24 different programs that are designed to help heal families through counseling, education, awareness, and support services.

All of the clinical and educational programs are focused on the child and cover three major areas: child abuse and family violence, parenting education, and anger management. Through counseling and education they address issues of family violence and how it affects both children and adults, helping families learn how to identify and deal with it while offering clients a protected venue for child visitations. Since a large percentage of their adult clients grew up in violent homes and many were abused themselves, they unknowingly pass these behaviors on to their children. The goal is to help these adults recognize and redefine their behaviors.

*The Exchange Club helps children who have been trau-
matized by abuse and violence to begin the healing process. Without the counseling and education offered at
the Center, regardless of whether they can pay or not,
these families would have nowhere else to go. Therefore
we know we are helping both generations overcome the
trauma and use of abuse and violence.*

Barbara King, The Exchange Club Family Center

Parenting education programs address the conflicts that arise
from stressful parenting situations and divorce. For example, TRANS-
parenting is a 4-hour seminar providing parents information on the
effects of divorce on children, while Rollercoasters is designed for the
children, who are also going through this traumatic family event and
are experiencing a wide range of emotions. Anger management programs address the issue of anger and explore alternative problem-solv-
ing skills, causes of anger, reactions to anger, and its aftereffects.

Serving over 5,500 children and adults with a team of 35 staff
is only possible through the amazing efforts of volunteers. The Family Center has become highly recognized for its partnership with
the AmeriCorps National Community Service Program and their
internships, which train graduate and undergraduate students from
numerous area colleges and universities. Playing our part in the
effort is easy, as well.

How can you give back? The Family Center is always in need
of children's toys, books, diapers, formula, and favors to celebrate
progress of children and teens. Consider adopting a family for holiday
gift giving, attending and volunteering with special events, or joining
a local Exchange Club, which provide support to the Family Center.

Learn more by visiting www.exhangeclub.net.

Chapter 51

SHELBY COUNTY BOOKS FROM BIRTH

Shelby County Books from Birth is a nonprofit whose mission is to bring Dolly Parton's Imagination Library to the residents of Shelby County. The organization secures funding to provide an age-appropriate book each month to children ages 0-5 that are registered in the program. Since their inception in 2005, more than 65,000 Shelby County children have enrolled in the program, and more than 1,000 new registrations are added each month, fueled by grassroots outreach in neighborhoods, child care centers and literacy groups.

I think it goes without saying for readers of this book, that reading to children is of paramount importance when it comes to building vocabulary, enhancing learning, preparing them for success in school, and strengthening the bond between parent and child. The more a parent talks and reads to their baby, the faster the child will learn. In fact, the report of the Commission on Reading states that "the single most important activity for building the knowledge required for eventual success in reading is reading aloud to children." Reading to a child also encourages them to associate reading with love and comfort.

More than half of the infants and preschoolers under the age of five in Shelby County grow up receiving, reading, and loving the same children's books, often the only ones in the home, mailed to them once a month by Books from Birth. We are honored to come alongside and be a part of helping parents in every single neighborhood as they raise their children.

Peter Abell, Shelby County Books from Birth

Providing a new book each month to children across Shelby County is a heroic feat. What is also impressive, from a business standpoint, is the cost per book is only $1. So, $12 provides books for one child for an entire year; and $60 provides books for a child for the full five years that the child is served by the program. Many families do not know that they can actually help the effort and enable the organization to reach more children by donating the $60. Either way, when it comes to making a huge difference in the life of a child, I think $12 or even $60 is a manageable amount for an individual or business to consider.

How can you give back? There are also a number of easy ways to help Shelby County Books from Birth through volunteerism. Volunteers are needed to follow up on voicemails, write thank you letters to donors and manage emails. They need help entering enrollees into the Imagination Library database, updating contact information for families, and coordinating with birthing centers to deliver brochures. Plenty of opportunities also exist to assist with community events and group projects.

Learn more about Shelby County Books from Birth by visiting their website at www.booksfrombirth.org or by contacting their Executive Director, Peter Abell, at pabell@booksfrombirth.org or 901-820-4501.

Chapter 52

JUVENILE INTERVENTION & FAITH-BASED FOLLOW-UP

Have you ever faced a crossroad? Giving back often means reaching into lives that are facing a crossroad. Juvenile Intervention & Faith-based Follow-up (JIFF) does just that. Every day, somewhere in Memphis, JIFF is reaching into young lives and delivering the opportunity for hope.

Founded by Reverend Rick Carr in 2003, JIFF targets youth ages 12-21 (and their families), who are involved in the juvenile justice system. JIFF works to break the destructive cycle of juvenile crime through faith-based intervention. These youth are primarily repeat offenders who are referred from the juvenile court for reentry or diversionary intervention services. In 2008, Tennessee quit funding the local incarceration of juvenile offenders in Memphis. All local juvenile detention centers were closed. The need for JIFF has only grown! Carr and his team are working with some of our city's youngest criminals and affording them a chance to turn their lives around, become productive citizens, and flourish free from a life of crime.

"Every day we are fighting to overcome evil with good. This is how we give back."

Reverend Rick Carr, JIFF

JIFF's program focuses on five key areas of a youth's life, in order to foster an inside-out transition. Focusing on Head, JIFF works on mental health and academic ability through various tutoring, GED training, assessments, and mentoring. Heart is core to teaching values and providing a foundation centered on Christ. Health fosters fitness training to teach discipline and routine, as well as promote self-image and worth. Hire-ability is taught through their Learn to Earn (LTE) program, which offers structured vocational classes, like Culinary Arts Training and Career Readiness. Home incorporates parents, teaching anger management, conflict resolution, and how to raise positive kids in a negative world.

JIFF has worked with over 650 youth and has a number of heartfelt success stories, like Jhukuruin Corley, who I recently met. Corley has turned his life around and is now a successful college student with a full-time job. Carr and his team exemplify how a positive force can affect the lives of these youth and, in turn, help our community lower the recidivism rate with juvenile offenders. In most cases, JIFF is enjoying rates below 35% with its graduates, which is astounding when you consider various national studies suggest a range of 50-80% for these individuals reoffending within three years.

How can you give back? Helping JIFF with their efforts is easy and fun. Start by taking a tour of their center, located at 254 South Lauderdale St. It is a remodeled YMCA that has quite a history — BB King recording his first hit song in their gymnasium. Then, sit down to a gourmet lunch made from scratch by youth at their culinary school. Your meal will be delicious and the personal stories from those who prepared it will be unforgettable! Consider volunteering by playing pool, ping-pong, or basketball with the kids. Or, call one of the kids once a week or send an email of encouragement.

Learn more by visiting www.jiffyouth.org or contacting Rick Carr at 901-522-8502 or rick@jiffyouth.org.

PERSPECTIVE THEMED

Chapter 53

TAKING A STAND WITH POSITIVES

There is a pesky misconception, especially in the world of media, that negative news travels further and faster than positive news. It goes back to the idea that someone will tell ten people about a bad experience versus only a few, if the experience is superb. Compound that with the mentality that "sensationalism sells" or "if it bleeds, it leads" and we have a sad recipe for disaster in our community where negative news starts to be sought out, glorified, and habitual, becoming an everyday focus and mindset.

However, I believe in the power of the positive. As Memphis moves into the next generation, positive energy and being intentional to share hope-filled and uplifting stories are the very things that will give us life. We need to celebrate our everyday heroes, those living and leading by example to make our city great!

Just like all things in life, the key to our success in Memphis is balance. It is important for the mental health of our community to balance investigative journalism and stories meant to raise awareness or invoke sadness with those that lift our spirits, celebrate positives, inspire us to do more and raise our expectations, and make us proud to live in our city and nation. Think of it like the weather. If we go a long duration without sunlight, our attitudes become agitated and eventually, apathetic. Once we step outside into the sunlight, though, our outlook becomes brighter, our energy elevates, and our ambitions begin to soar.

FedEx gives back in a number of ways on a local, national and global level. We do this through things like direct corporate contributions, in-kind shipping, volunteer work by our employees and more to help bring about positive change in communities around the world. Being a good corporate citizen is extremely important to the company, and you can find out more about the number of ways in which FedEx gives back by visiting www.fedexcares.com.

Richard Smith, FedEx

While many business leaders are engaged in the community and have a chance to see the good taking place every day here in the Mid-South, most Memphians and especially college students and tourists, have no knowledge of where to turn. So, this is where we need to take our stand! This is where we need to lead by example and show fellow Memphians and visitors the real heart and soul of our city by being intentional, everyday, to share positive energy and direct them to those outlets and stories. Let us make it extremely easy and overly accessible to see the good in Memphis!

Think of it as giving back to your city and the request is amazingly simple: just spread good news! We need anyone and everyone to help create a pipeline of positive stories that the news outlets can share. We need to sing from the rooftops, using social media channels to promote things that will make us smile, even if for a second. We need to show the world, and most importantly, our kids, that we care and want to inspire and be inspired. Let us take a stand with positives!

Chapter 54

COMMUNITY TIES INTO ELEVATOR PITCH

A llow me to share a few tips that can help us refine our story and elevator pitches. An elevator pitch is basically a short summary of who you are, what you have done or what you are doing, and how that adds value. Since the term derives from the challenge of explaining your business or fit for a potential job in the short amount of time it takes to get from one floor to another in an elevator, think of it as a purposeful tool for communicating core information quickly that can lead to an invitation to have a longer conversation down the road.

Just think, the first question usually asked at events or job interviews is "Tell me about yourself" or "What do you do?" With either question, the goal is to spark a conversation. So, the idea is to provide a teaser that draws them in, tells a piece of your story, and most importantly, connects the dots on why it benefits them or their organization. Think of it as quick, 30 to 60 second sound bites (the attention span of most business leaders nowadays), where you can promote your best skills or experiences and tie them back with relevance to the other person, situation, or opportunity.

Generally, some of the top tips with elevator pitches are to use the simplest language possible, avoid speaking the way you write, turn your pitch into a question, and sometimes ditch the "pitch" all together.

To take those a step further, pick three specific things that make you unique, like talents, experiences, trips, and languages. For each, have a story that illustrates a "value" and is programmed to recite on command in very short or longer versions. Many leaders and public speakers have amazing stories, but what makes them so marketable is that they can instantly share their stories in whatever timeframe is appropriate. Their stories and lessons can be shared in 30 seconds, two minutes, or two hour versions, if the situation and audience fits.

> *The employees at Vaco seek out opportunities to serve in community leadership positions. We know giving of our time and talents to nonprofit organizations makes our city a better place to live.*
>
> Cheryl Citrone, Vaco

We talk about it often, but if you ask any leader what is most important, aside from their business and family, community tops the list. For this reason, your community efforts offer a perfect platform to stand out. The key is to highlight "leadership" roles you are taking, along with the impact of your efforts and how they are helping others in the Mid-South. It is great to be giving back, but even better to be leading an effort in some way. So, make sure to have one or two stories that illustrate your community engagement that you can use as a conversation spark.

Know your sphere of influence and how everyone is interconnected. Memphis is a large city, but once you connect people with their passions, it quickly shrinks to a close-knit, almost family-like environment. Do your homework before going to an event or interview, so you know something about the people you will be meeting. Talk to the "wallflowers" because many times, it is a CEO standing back and analyzing the situation. Lastly, practice a lot (video yourself) and remember to SMILE because that positive energy is contagious!

Chapter 55

LEGACY STATEMENT

A legacy statement, which is somewhat of an ancient tradition, is a personal message that captures the significance of one's life. Legacy statements can be a lasting imprint from a corporate leader or a heartfelt note from parent to child, but the idea is to share stories that defined and shaped the principles and beliefs by which you lived your life or ran your business. It is not about archiving achievements, but describing moments that revealed character and what you deemed most important.

There are numerous tips online for crafting a legacy statement. First, sit down and reflect upon your life, thinking about your belief system and what morals you might pass along. Introduce yourself and paint a picture of your life for those who might not have ever known or met you, while crafting your message to a specific audience, like family or employees. Be honest and provide your wisdom and advice, so that people can learn from your successes and failures. Lastly, use the legacy statement as a chance to share your love and let others know how much you cared for them.

> *masterIT believes in our community. Our clients, team members and partners live here and contribute to our success, so we feel we have a vested interest in giving back. As a team we participate in non-profit functions*

dear to us, and they give us the opportunity to work together for the good of others in need. It has become part of who we are.

Michael Drake, masterIT

Even though a legacy statement may seem like something that should wait until retirement, there is no better time than now to start thinking about the legacy you want to leave behind. In defining your legacy statement now, you are affording yourself the opportunity to take control, create it, and live it out, versus having to glance back later in life, perhaps with regrets. A past LPBC guest speaker, Wes Moore, said it best: "When it's time for you to leave, make sure that it mattered you were even here." The more you can define now, such as your priorities and goals, the more "it mattered" will take care of itself.

Recently, I lost two uncles to different types of cancer. Both were rocks in our family and will be forever missed. While I will always have amazing memories, I wish each of them would have crafted a legacy statement for us to cherish and share with future generations of our family. It would have been a great gift to know what they prized and held in high regard. The older I get, the more I appreciate learning from others, which teaches us more about ourselves. So, although we might not have control of our "time to leave," we can definitely make the most of each day and work to leave a lasting impression through our legacy statement.

Chapter 56

ENGAGING EMPLOYEES
IN THE COMMUNITY

This past year, we were honored to have Richard Montañez, who is the famous janitor that invented Flamin' Hot Cheetos and now leads Multicultural Sales and Community Promotions for PepsiCo's North America Divisions as their top Latino executive, speak at our Lipscomb Pitts Breakfast Club. It was an inspiring morning with a host of business and community leaders from across the Mid-South. Part of the message Richard delivered was an echo of the theme we discuss each week through the "Giving Back" columns — corporate philanthropy focusing on engagement, noting that customers and employees alike are more and more expecting corporations to be directly involved within their communities. This means community engagement is truly becoming a fundamental component of corporate sustainability.

For business leaders, the key is finding simple, yet meaningful ways to create opportunities for employees, who are the real brand ambassadors, to give back in the community. Since most employees genuinely welcome an opportunity to support nonprofits and help our city, leaders must provide them with the encouragement, freedom, and support to do so. Below are three ways companies can manage the weekly workload, but also incentivize their teams to roll up their sleeves and make a "hands on" impact.

First, allow employees to modify their work schedule. Since many volunteer opportunities can fit within a workday, like tutoring youth afterschool from 3:30p-5:00p, allowing employees to adjust their schedule provides an encouraging solution. Companies may allow employees to shift their day forward, so no time is lost, or make up the difference on another day. As another option, companies could provide a certain amount of time per month or year that may be allotted for corporate-endorsed volunteer days.

> *We believe that along with our success comes the fundamental responsibility to make a positive contribution to the community. Our business meets this responsibility through a combination of financial and product contributions, by encouraging leadership by example and supporting employee participation in volunteer activities.*
>
> Dave Carlson, Smith & Nephew

Second, tie active engagement to corporate sponsorships. Companies usually encourage employees to take leadership roles with nonprofits, like serving on boards or on steering committees. To show support, the company will then make the commitment to sponsor those nonprofit events in which the employee is participating. Tying corporate sponsorships to employee engagement shows support, offers encouragement, and also affords the employee a chance to strengthen their leadership skills. The nonprofit receives personal and financial support, and the company receives marketing and community goodwill, as well.

Third, tie corporate donations to volunteer hours spent at a nonprofit. There are many variations, but a basic example is if an employee donates 10 personal hours of service, the company will match the effort with a $500 donation on their behalf. Some companies will give employees an amount per year, like $1,000, which they can contribute based where they are actively volunteering.

These are just three examples to get your creative juices flowing. I encourage you to look at ways you can motivate and allow your employees to get more engaged and create your own opportunities to give back.

Chapter 57

GIVING BACK FOR GROWTH?

If Memphis is going to be a vibrant community - where we retain and attract the best talent, grow industry, and enrich the quality of life for our families — everyone needs to take part in the effort. Each of us needs to take ownership and have the pride to not turn our back, which never solves anything, but to commit resources, albeit time or money, to being a part of the solution. The beauty is that together we can each make a difference and change the world with simple, daily steps.

This concept has been the focus of my *Giving Back* column since its inception. In a world where money is tight, jobs scarce, and skepticism still prevalent, let us explore three ways giving back can get you ahead.

First is storytelling. In an era where trust and engagement are critical, companies are moving toward interactive conversations with team members and their communities. Individuals are shifting from bullet-point resumes to biographies that reflect character and offer perspective. Being actively engaged in the community gives you a unique storyline. This community-focused storyline is both critical as a business and as an individual searching for a job or trying to stand out in today's competitive workplace.

Service allows you to experience a way of investing in your own well-being while impacting the community or the life of another. It is surprising the numbers of doors that will open to a servant...and behind those doors are hearts of gold. This is where the most meaningful relationships are sparked.

Allison Carson, Lipscomb & Pitts Insurance

Second, your opportunities in life come from other people. Ask any business leader what is paramount outside of their business and community engagement will top the list. Business leaders understand the role the community plays in their company's success from economic, human capital, and even intrinsic levels. If you want to find common ground and associate with these business leaders — who may present you with opportunities — getting engaged in a nonprofit gives you the perfect platform.

Third is personal and professional growth. Working with a nonprofit allows you to sharpen your leadership skills and showcase your expertise. In the process of volunteering or leading a project, you are honing your skills and building trust with business leaders and the nonprofit. Similar to a college internship, you have a chance to work with a group of people toward a shared goal, and shine in the process. There have been many recent success stories with nonprofits hiring volunteers or companies hiring someone, who was volunteering with an affiliated nonprofit.

Giving back will always be the right thing to do, but it does not hurt to look at how and why weaving community engagement into your business and life routine is a good growth strategy.

Chapter 58

SMALL ACTIONS START MOVEMENTS

I am always amazed at the power of small beginnings. Small actions can lead to gigantic movements! Back in 2011, one of our Lipscomb Pitts Breakfast Club (LPBC) guest speakers was Chad Pregracke, founder of Living Lands & Waters, which is a nonprofit dedicated to cleaning up our nation's waterways. Over the last 14 years, Chad and his team have worked with hundreds of cities and towns and over 70,000 volunteers in 18 states to remove over 7 million pounds of garbage. They have done it one piece at a time, one river at a time.

Chad Pregracke started a movement by seeing a problem in his community and simply taking action. Chad notes, "I'm just a regular guy who saw a problem and wanted to do something about it." While working through college, Chad camped out on the banks of the rivers and saw trash everywhere. After personally lobbying for a cleanup, he decided to do it himself. His relentless dedication and passion has created a multi-million dollar cleanup business, which attracts tens of thousands of volunteers each year to help the effort and draw awareness for clean water and environmental sustainability.

It started with seeing a problem and taking action. Locally, we are seeing this same community self-start attitude take shape. LPBC partner, Phelps Security (Lloyd@phelpssecurity.com), recently started BIG (Business Interest Group) for Memphis to bring Colonels with the Memphis Police Department together with business leaders to share Blue CRUSH presentations and crime prevention information. The group is now tackling action projects, like having more than 30 volunteers paint over graffiti on the railroad bridge over Ridgeway at Park.

As another example, Colton Cockrum at the University of Memphis (ccockrum@memphis.edu), has teamed up with Memphis City Beautiful to coordinate cleanup efforts at McKeller Lake. Colton took part in the original Living Lands & Waters cleanup back in 2011 and saw how badly the area needed attention. To date, hundreds of volunteers have helped remove almost 50,000 pounds of trash from McKellar Lake and the effort both continues and has expanded to include the banks of the mighty Mississippi River.

> *The University of Memphis provides opportunities for students, faculty, and staff to get involved in our community. Our students are placed into opportunities for giving back and subsequently take the lead on important community issues.*
>
> Dr. Colton Cockrum, University of Memphis

These are just simple examples of how individuals and companies are stepping up in their own way to be a part of the solution for our community. They see something that needs to be done and are taking it upon themselves to do the job. These small steps are what we need to start movements. My commitment is to help these efforts and focus resources their way, so that we can make them stronger. My hope is that you will join me and also start looking for ways you can take small daily steps to make our community better.

Chapter 59

CORPORATIONS CRITICAL TO COMMUNITY SUCCESS

C orporations have always played an integral role in the economic and social fabric of America. The two are inherently intertwined. Consider local examples, like FedEx Corporation, AutoZone, Smith & Nephew, Baptist Memorial Health Care, and International Paper to name a few. Businesses provide infrastructure and opportunity through job creation, goods and services, financial stimulus, attracting additional investment, philanthropy, and more. Respectively, business leaders understand the role community plays in their company's success from economic, human capital, and intrinsic levels.

Although the success of a company has never been measured by the success of its community and it has never been a prerequisite to be engaged, the tides are rapidly turning. Consumers now expect businesses to be actively engaged and a part of the solution, not just a good citizen. This shift in expectations has recently made headlines among national newspapers and periodicals. Personally, I will take it a step further and say that consumer expectations are redefining "corporate philanthropy." The new definition extends beyond donations to now include social activation with volunteerism and projects or programs that provide strategic impact.

Through financial support, employee engagement and civic leadership, AutoZone invests in education, social services, health and wellness, economic development and the arts to build a promising future.

AutoZone

Part of this phenomenon is the world we live in and the challenges we face, but the key is consumers understand that businesses have more resources, both financial and human, that they can leverage for the greater good. A company's impact thus becomes a differentiator for customers to make purchasing decisions. Perhaps the most noticeable indicator is online, where consumers are leveraging social media to research impact and share their findings with the world.

Type "Made in USA" in any search engine and hundreds of websites, blogs, and books pop up that are devoted to promoting products made in the States. What has always been a source of pride and campaign to "buy local," is now our national symbol for retaining and cultivating jobs and stimulating our economy. This same approach of supporting local businesses and keeping our money in the Mid-South is firmly taking hold locally, as well. Each day, we hear stories of customers actively trying to support companies that are giving back and supporting the community. Even small purchases reflect the sentiment, like recently I purchased soap based on proceeds benefiting St. Jude Children's Research Hospital.

Community engagement is now one of the key elements for corporate sustainability and success. Understanding this shift in consumer expectations is critical. The fun then becomes weaving giving back into your normal routine and being creative, which will open up a whole new world of possibilities for you, your company, and our community.

Chapter 60

PROMOTIONS BENEFITING NONPROFITS AND BUSINESSES

Giving back is always the right thing to do and is a positive for our community, but let us be realistic in that corporations want and need to leverage their engagement. Business leaders make their living on Return on Investment (ROI). So, finding opportunities that support nonprofits and yield positive effects for a business are opportunities that will be long-lived and fruitful.

One tried and true formula is tying in a nonprofit with your own special promotion. There are many different variations, ranging from a percentage of sales being donated to leading a campaign that collects money or goods. A recent example would be the "Pass-A-Pepper for Hope" Program with national restaurant chain Chili's Grill & Bar donating 100 percent of their net profits on "The Big Day," September 26, to our local St. Jude Children's Research Hospital. According to friends at St. Jude, not only has this annual promotion (in its eighth year) helped raise over $35 million dollars for the pediatric cancer hospital, it has also benefited Chili's with increased dining traffic, customer loyalty, and even increases in stock value.

*I believe locally owned and operated businesses are what
define a city. My business is in the service industry. I commit my business, time, and resources to dozens of fund*

raising projects a year. I also like to create my own, like the "Heart Full of Soul" multi-sensory dinners that benefits The Stax Music Academy. Serving others is not just my purpose in life — it's the reason for my existence.

Glenda Hastings, Napa Café

Carrying this example forward, Chili's used social media, like Facebook and Twitter, to interact with guests and provide them more information and ways to donate. Guests could sign up for Chili's Email Club to receive special offers and follow the hash tag, #CreateAPepper, to show support and see how others were spreading hope for St. Jude. What an impressive opportunity to strengthen the relationship with customers, reach new ones through a shared passion for St. Jude, and carry it forward, so that it generates repeat business.

Locally, you can create this same type of promotional opportunity by teaming with your favorite nonprofit for a day, a month, or even a full year. Great local restaurants like Napa Café have adopted this concept, developing themed evenings to benefit local charities. The partnership between local restaurants and local nonprofits is a truly effective combination. Perhaps 10 percent of net profits or 15 percent of total purchases will benefit the organization. Or take the route of collecting goods, like if customers bring in canned goods for the Mid-South Food Bank's Operation Feed, they will receive 10 percent off a purchase. Simply leading an effort to collect goods or money is also a terrific option.

The point is that you go the extra mile to create your own campaign. This allows you to brand the campaign with your business, strengthen the bond with your customers, and showcase your commitment to the community. It gives you a great reason to leverage social media and other marketing channels, as well as potentially reach new customers by having your supported nonprofit promote the campaign, too. What a perfect win-win!

Chapter 61

BENEFICIAL WATCH PARTY

The "beneficial watch party" is a time-tested favorite when it comes to weaving giving back into your everyday life. Every weekend now presents a prime opportunity to have fun watching your favorite games while easily and effectively raising money and awareness for a nonprofit you support. The plan is simple: host a watch party at your house and invite your family and friends, telling them in advance that the event will benefit your selected nonprofit. As host, you provide the normal food and drinks, but ask attendees to consider donating what they would typically spend on lunch or dinner to the nonprofit. You will be pleasantly surprised how much money one of these events can raise. It will also warm your heart knowing that whether your team wins or loses, your event is a true victory in blessing others.

These watch parties are perfect for football and basketball games, any type of television show or awards show, or even a movie night at your house. You can also apply this same concept to a birthday party, backyard cookout, or swim party. The exciting thing is that a "beneficial watch party" works well with everyone at all ages. I have heard great success stories with families and college students equally raising hundreds and even thousands of dollars by hosting these types of events. In fact, one friend who has been hosting these over the last two years throughout the entire football season has already been able to raise and contribute over $10,000!

Simply Delicious looks for every opportunity to give back to our amazing community. Every week, we donate food to non-profit organizations asking for help. We take the time to connect with our clients on a personal level and help them help the community through food and service. We have a long way to go to achieve what I believe is the "ultimate us" in giving to our community, but we are well on our way to that place!

Tricia Woodman, Simply Delicious Catering

Just as important, know that you are also helping to raise general awareness for the organization. Having some literature on hand, directing your family and friends to a website, and personally sharing your story or testimonial on why you selected the nonprofit will open great doors of possibilities for the future. The other key is that you are acting as a role model and encouraging others to do something similar where they can weave giving back into their normal day and life.

So, as you start planning upcoming events, consider helping others by hosting your own "beneficial watch party."

Chapter 62

WE ALL PLAY A PART IN RETAINING TALENT

Memphis boasts a wealth of vibrant and accomplished colleges and universities. Our schools have long received national acclaim for strong programs and outstanding academic achievement. However, our business and community leaders have also been stepping up to focus on the important task of attracting, developing, and retaining talent. This collaborative spirit is the recipe for success in Memphis.

We have discussed this topic before and highlighted certain organizations for the role they are playing in the effort. As a community, we must realize that we are only as strong as our leaders and the conviction and pride we all have for our city. Ideas and vision are today's currency and, in a world rapidly driven by technology, knowledge workers and college educated employees set the stage for growth and development. We all win when we can attract global talent, develop our tremendous potential, and then retain individuals with opportunities to succeed.

This was evidenced recently at the New Memphis Institute's Boardof Governors Meeting, where the economic impact of retaining around 800 knowledge workers in Memphis was estimated at over $54.5 million. That number is just the economic impact, not even factoring the social benefits derived from their civic engagement and leadership.

Thanks to the many great organizations, educational institutions, companies, and individuals focused on this effort. Kudos to Mayor Wharton for being innovative and launching the Office of Talent and Human Capital, led by Dr. Douglas Scarboro, which is focused on this initiative. We have spotlighted groups, like the New Memphis Institute, Leadership Memphis, the University of Memphis and their LEAD, MILE, and Academic Internship programs. Our public, charter, and private schools play a key role not only in developing our future leaders, but also attracting world class teachers and talent.

> *We support the organizations that our employees support, whether through sponsorships or volunteering. CBRE Memphis employees are represented on more than 25 Boards of Directors, allowing us to make our city stronger. Memphis is a great place to live and we are proud to be a part of it. Let's all do our part to encourage other people to move to Memphis and be a part of our family.*
>
> J. Kevin Adams, CB Richard Ellis Memphis

The key is to realize that no one group can do it alone and it takes each of us doing our part for Memphis to succeed. We need business leaders to step foot onto school campuses and let students know they are needed — that we want them to stay and will do what it takes to keep them here and show them opportunities. There is a "disconnect" between the momentum and opportunities we see and what students think exist. It is up to us to change that "disconnect."

Just as critical, when new families relocate or move to Memphis, we need to personally help them engage. We need to refer them to organizations, like mentioned above, that have pipelines and resources to help. Our job is to make it easy and understand we each play a part with our actions and words. So, let's make them count!

NOTES

NOTES

NOTES